Heavy Laden

The psychological aftereffects of war are not just a modern-day plight. Following the Civil War, numerous soldiers returned with damaged bodies or damaged minds. Drawing on archival materials, including digitized records for more than 70,000 white and African American Union army recruits, newspaper reports, and census returns, Larry M. Logue and Peter Blanck uncover the diversity and severity of Civil War veterans' psychological distress. Their findings concerning the recognition of veterans' post-traumatic stress disorders, treatment programs, and suicide rates will inform current studies on how to effectively cope with this enduring disability in former soldiers. This compelling book brings to light the continued sacrifices of men who went to war.

Larry M. Logue is Senior Fellow at the Burton Blatt Institute at Syracuse University. He received a PhD in American Civilization from the University of Pennsylvania. His books include *To Appomattox and Beyond: The Civil War Soldier in War and Peace* and *Race, Ethnicity, and Disability: Veterans and Benefits in Post-Civil War America*, coauthored with Peter Blanck.

Peter Blanck is University Professor at Syracuse University and Chairman of the Burton Blatt Institute. He received a Juris Doctorate from Stanford University, where he was president of the *Stanford Law Review*, and a PhD in Social Psychology from Harvard University. His recent books include *Routledge Handbook of Disability Law and Human Rights*, coedited with Eilionóir Flynn, and *eQuality: The Struggle for Web Accessibility by People with Cognitive Disabilities*.

CAMBRIDGE DISABILITY LAW AND POLICY SERIES

Edited by
Peter Blanck and Robin Paul Malloy

The Disability Law and Policy series examines these topics in interdisciplinary and comparative terms. The books in the series reflect the diversity of definitions, causes, and consequences of discrimination against persons with disabilities while illuminating fundamental themes that unite countries in their pursuit of human rights laws and policies to improve the social and economic status of persons with disabilities. The series contains historical, contemporary, and comparative scholarship crucial to identifying individual, organizational, cultural, attitudinal, and legal themes necessary for the advancement of disability law and policy.

The book topics covered in the series also are reflective of the new moral and political commitment by countries throughout the world toward equal opportunity for persons with disabilities in such areas as employment, housing, transportation, rehabilitation, and individual human rights. The series will thus play a significant role in informing policy makers, researchers, and citizens of issues central to disability rights and disability antidiscrimination policies. The series grounds the future of disability law and policy as a vehicle for ensuring that those living with disabilities participate as equal citizens of the world.

Heavy Laden

Union Veterans, Psychological Illness, and Suicide

LARRY M. LOGUE
PETER BLANCK

Syracuse University

With a Foreword by Elyn Saks

CAMBRIDGE
UNIVERSITY PRESS

CAMBRIDGE
UNIVERSITY PRESS

University Printing House, Cambridge CB2 8BS, United Kingdom

One Liberty Plaza, 20th Floor, New York, NY 10006, USA

477 Williamstown Road, Port Melbourne, VIC 3207, Australia

314-321, 3rd Floor, Plot 3, Splendor Forum, Jasola District Centre, New Delhi - 110025, India

79 Anson Road, #06-04/06, Singapore 079906

Cambridge University Press is part of the University of Cambridge.

It furthers the University's mission by disseminating knowledge in the pursuit of education, learning and research at the highest international levels of excellence.

www.cambridge.org
Information on this title: www.cambridge.org/9781107589957
DOI: 10.1017/9781316459782

First published 2018
First paperback edition 2019

A catalogue record for this publication is available from the British Library

ISBN 978-1-107-13349-5 Hardback
ISBN 978-1-107-58995-7 Paperback

Come unto him – all ye that Labour, come unto him that
are heavy laden, and he will give you Rest.

     – George Frideric Handel, "He Shall Feed His Flock,"
     Messiah (manuscript courtesy of Pierpont Morgan
     Library Department of Music Manuscripts
     and Books)

Contents

Contents

Figures

List of Figures

Tables

List of Tables

Foreword

"I have a major mental illness...If you are a person with mental illness, the challenge is to find the life that's right for you. But in truth, isn't that the challenge for all of us, mentally ill or not?" In my 2007 memoir, *The Center Cannot Hold: My Journey through Madness*, I wrote these words. Although I have been fortunate to receive for my work on mental illness numerous honors, including a 2009 John D. and Catherine T. MacArthur Fellowship (the so-called Genius Grant), in many ways, the memoir was my "coming out" as a person with schizophrenia.

Yet, despite the voluminous writings on the medicalization of mental illness, it is still difficult to grasp the very personal nature of the mind's operation. Fixing a line beyond which lies psychosis is difficult. How do we distinguish difference, or eccentricity, from frank medical illness?

The study of suicide is similarly contested: the act is easier to define, but its inducements remain persistently elusive. If this is the case today, what is to be gained from investigating the US Civil War era, when masturbation was considered a major cause of mental illness and overcivilization was blamed for suicides?

Heavy Laden offers a compelling answer. The book takes its place in the lively debate about the fate of military veterans past and present. Mental illness and suicide among veterans are grave concerns in our own time; some historians have pointed to parallel symptoms among Civil War soldiers and veterans, while others contend that reading present issues into the past misrepresents ex-soldiers' readjustment. Larry M. Logue and Peter Blanck take a fresh approach to the debate. They use data from Union army veterans to explore tendencies toward mental illness and suicide, complementing this information with testimony from veterans themselves.

Logue and Blanck's approach then weaves individual case examples into a more systematic narrative of Civil War suicides. The approach, that is, provides both individual stories that grab the reader and more extensive, quantitative data comparing different groups around suicide, which put the individual stories into a richer context.

The authors recognize the need to consider the past on its own terms. Designations such as insanity, melancholia, and irritable heart have changed or disappeared since the nineteenth century. Translation of past diagnoses can be frustrating, but Logue and Blanck adopt a different tack. They make comparisons with civilians, as in the increased concealment of veterans' "insanity" from census-takers. The authors also compare the races, as in African Americans' greater reluctance to claim insanity in medical examinations for pensions.

Though the past was its own world, it retains links to our time. Logue and Blanck present a telling comparison between Union veterans' suicide rate in Massachusetts and that of ex-soldiers in 2014. Surprisingly, given the likely greater stigma against suicide then, the nineteenth-century rate was higher; perhaps treatment is better now. The authors thoroughly explore the implications of this finding, which brings the relationship between past and present into sharper focus. This book opens new scholarly dimensions and unique benchmarks for considering earlier veterans' so-called nervous afflictions.

Logue and Blanck's work here also builds upon and extends their 2010 book *Race, Ethnicity, and Disability: Veterans and Benefits in Post–Civil War America*, which was another seminal investigation of discrimination in the Civil War pension system as experienced by Union army veterans with differing disabilities and ethnicities, and by African Americans. Once again, Logue and Blanck offer groundbreaking analyses and insights of how veterans across the spectrum of humanity perceived and coped with warfare's consequences. Logue and Blanck brilliantly open up new historical vistas, reminding me of the promise by which I closed *The Center Cannot Hold*: "the humanity we all share is more important than the mental illness we may not."

Elyn Saks

Acknowledgments

We would hardly say that our project was light work, but we will gladly confirm that it profited from the help of many hands. Our exploration of primary sources was aided by Jack Eckert of the Countway Medical Library at Harvard University; William Creech of the National Archives staff; Noelle Yetter of the Early Indicators project; Gilbert Abbe of the Genealogical Society of Utah's Family History Library; and Mary Killeen, Philip Ross, and Diana Foote of the Burton Blatt Institute at Syracuse University.

Burton Blatt Institute staff members were also willing and able participants in manuscript preparation. We are especially grateful to William Myhill, Jack Cronin, DaThao Nguyen, and Michelle Woodhouse. Celestia Ohrazda and Sally Weiss helped us obtain feedback for our findings.

Acknowledgments

The program of research for this project is supported, in part, by grants to the Burton Blatt Institute; information is available at http://bbi.syr.edu. We also deeply appreciate comments on our manuscript by Eric Dean and Jay Winter.

Our families helped in ways that eclipse mere acknowledgments. Barbara Logue's contribution as life coach, patient listener, and constructive critic has been inestimable. Bertha and Albert A. Blanck, no longer alive, and Wendy, Jason, Elise, Daniel, Albert, Caroline, and Harry Blanck are the sun around which all Peter Blanck's life endeavors revolve.

A portion of Chapter 2 was originally published as Larry M. Logue, "Elephants and Epistemology: Evidence of Suicide in the Gilded Age," *Journal of Social History* 49 (2015): 374–386. It is used here with the permission of Oxford University Press.

Introduction

The study of Civil War veterans has been a stepchild of scholarship on soldiering. It could scarcely have been otherwise: the singular event that produced a mountain of participants' testimony carries more urgency than do the seemingly amorphous experiences of ex-soldiers. By the end of the twentieth century, historians of soldiering in the Civil War had developed that hallmark of a field's maturity, an interpretive controversy. Did the accumulated horrors of warfare embitter the men who served, or did their immanent patriotism see them through the ordeal? Scholars have taken positions on one side or the other of this question.[1]

---

[1] For overviews that describe the debate and guide readers to relevant works, see Reid Mitchell, "'Not the General but the Soldier':

But research on veterans has caught up. Early studies concentrated on public policy and organized activities, but in recent years more historians have focused on the experience of veterans themselves. This development was influenced by social historians' interest in ordinary people, but it also reflects the current solicitude for veterans of twenty-first-century conflicts. This connection has given veterans' history a controversy of its own. The essential issue is presentism, the imposition of today's judgments on interpretations of the past. Several studies of Civil War veterans have found evidence that corresponds to posttraumatic stress disorder, commonly known as PTSD. Critics contend, however, that foregrounding psychological damage imposes current antiwar sentiments on an era that did not share them and on the majority of veterans who did not suffer the damage. According to one critique, "readers who do not know much about the war might infer that atypical experiences were in fact normative ones."[2]

The Study of Civil War Soldiers," in James M. McPherson and William J. Cooper, eds., *Writing the Civil War: The Quest to Understand* (Columbia: University of South Carolina Press, 1998), 81–95; Michael Barton and Larry M. Logue, "The Soldiers and the Scholars," in Barton and Logue, eds., *The Civil War Soldier: A Historical Reader* (New York: New York University Press, 2002), 1–5; Aaron Sheehan-Dean, "The Blue and the Gray in Black and White: Assessing the Scholarship on Civil War Soldiers," in Aaron Sheehan-Dean, ed., *The View from the Ground: Experiences of Civil War Soldiers* (Lexington: University Press of Kentucky, 2007), 9–30.

[2] Gary W. Gallagher and Kathryn Shively Meier, "Coming to Terms with Civil War Military History," *Journal of the Civil War Era* 4

We take seriously the conflicting judgments about veterans and their fate. As with most debates, each side has virtues and flaws; the challenge is sorting out which is which. As in most disputes, one's first step implies a taking of

---

(2014), 492. On the evolution of veterans' studies, see Larry M. Logue and Michael Barton, *The Civil War Veteran: A Historical Reader* (New York: New York University Press, 2007), 1–6; Robert Cook, "The Quarrel Forgotten? Toward a Clearer Understanding of Sectional Reconciliation," *Journal of the Civil War Era* 6 (2016), 413–436. Studies that find psychological trauma among Civil War veterans include Diane M. Sommerville, "'Will They Ever Be Able to Forget?': Confederate Soldiers and Mental Illness in the Defeated South," in Stephen Berry, ed., *Weirding the War: Stories from the Civil War's Ragged Edges* (Athens: University of Georgia Press, 2011), 321–339; Eric T. Dean Jr., *Shook over Hell: Post-Traumatic Stress, Vietnam, and the Civil War* (Cambridge, MA: Harvard University Press, 1997); Katherine K. Ziff, *Asylum on the Hill: History of a Healing Landscape* (Athens: Ohio University Press, 2012), 19, 40–41; Michael C. C. Adams, *Living Hell: The Dark Side of the Civil War* (Baltimore: Johns Hopkins University Press, 2014); Diane M. Sommerville, "'A Burden Too Heavy to Bear': War Trauma, Suicide, and Confederate Soldiers," *Civil War History* 59 (2013), 453–491; Michael W. Schaefer, "'Really, Though, I'm Fine': Civil War Veterans and the Psychological Aftereffects of Killing," in Lawrence A. Kreiser and Randal Allred, eds., *The Civil War in Popular Culture: Memory and Meaning* (Lexington: University Press of Kentucky, 2014), 11–23; Eric T. Dean Jr., "Reflections on 'The Trauma of War' and *Shook over Hell*," *Civil War History* 59 (2013), 414–418. For other criticisms of recent soldiers' and veterans' history, see Yael A. Sternhell, "Revisionism Reinvented? The Antiwar Turn in Civil War Scholarship," *Journal of the Civil War Era* 3 (2013), 239–256; Wayne Wei-Siang Hsieh, "'Go to Your Gawd Like a Soldier': Transnational Reflections on Veteranhood," *Journal of the Civil War Era* 5 (2015), 551–577.

sides. Our first step in *Heavy Laden* is a focus on Union veterans' psychological disorders, but we appreciate the skepticism urged by critics. Their implication of presentism carries weight, and we address it in two ways. The obvious approach is to attend to context, to recognize the distant and different world in which Union veterans lived. In this study we make every effort to evoke the forms in which veterans and their communities understood mental illness and suicide.

But presentism can be evaluated as well as mitigated. A central goal of this study is to appraise the incidence of veterans' psychological disorders and suicides, partly in response to contemporary insinuations about the past. The coining of PTSD was accompanied by assertions that its symptoms were unique to Vietnam veterans, a notion that was demolished by a study of Civil War veterans in an Indiana insane asylum. The uniqueness claim has receded, but the assumption remains that recent wars have generated unprecedented amounts of psychological distress. Admitting that some posttraumatic stress is common to all wars, one writer sums up the prevailing presumption:

> Today, warfare has become more deadly, debilitating, and "invisible" than ever. This is due to the high numbers of available combatants around the world; the transformation of civilians into acceptable targets; and modern weapons that inevitably kill civilians, destroy infrastructure, poison the environment, annihilate millions in a blow, and can strike anywhere on the planet without even being manned.

We can surmise that the greater the destructive reach of our weaponry, the greater the moral stress and burden on troops and the nation, and the more penetrating yet mysterious the invisible wound will be.

This assertion is convertible into a question: Did a war that seemingly had less of this devastating force produce less postwar mental illness and suicide?[3]

[3] On coining PTSD and the Indiana evidence that refuted the Vietnam War's uniqueness, see Dean, *Shook over Hell,* 180–209; Dean, "Reflections." See also works cited in note 2. Quote from Edward Tick, *Warrior's Return: Restoring the Soul after War* (Boulder, CO: Sounds True, 2014), 102. Paul A. Cimbala makes a point related to this paragraph's topic, though with an inverted argument. Cimbala cautions about a focus on Civil War veterans' mental illnesses, suggesting that "research now beyond the expertise of most historians might very well complicate how scholars judge and assess Civil War trauma" (Paul A. Cimbala, *Veterans North and South: The Transition from Soldier to Civilian after the American Civil War* [Santa Barbara, CA: Praeger, 2015], xv). This caveat would carry more weight if the research were not riven by doubts about what PTSD is, how it manifests itself, and how common it is. For a sampling of the uncertainty that surrounds PTSD research, see James C. Jackson et al., "Variation in Practices and Attitudes of Clinicians Assessing PTSD-Related Disability among Veterans," *Journal of Traumatic Stress* 24 (2011), 609–613; Lisa K. Richardson, B. Christopher Frueh, and Ronald Acierno, "Prevalence Estimates of Combat-Related Post-Traumatic Stress Disorder: Critical Review," *Australian and New Zealand Journal of Psychiatry* 44 (2010), 4–19; Josefin Sundin et al., "PTSD after Deployment to Iraq: Conflicting Rates, Conflicting Claims," *Psychological Medicine* 40 (2010), 367–382; Richard J. McNally, "Progress and Controversy in the Study of Posttraumatic Stress Disorder," *Annual Review of Psychology* 54

Introduction

Some of the immoderate claims about current wars may come from conflating the two meanings of "incomparability." Because conditions of combat are not directly comparable between present and former conflicts, the current prevalence must be beyond compare. We are not so certain. Strict comparability is out of the question, but the context of the late nineteenth century offers a guide to assessing the surmise expressed in the above quote.

Critics' objection to slighting veterans' readjustment also deserves a fair hearing. Chapters 1, 2, and 3 are largely devoted to examining readjustment from multiple perspectives. They indicate that drawing a sharp line between "readjusted" and "troubled" veterans is unrealistic at any given time, and made more problematic as circumstances shifted over the decades. A skeptic might nonetheless point out that all the psychological disorders and suicides taken together affected nowhere near a majority of Union veterans. This is, however, a quantitative claim without an anchor. It implies a threshold of 50 percent for significance, but why is this preferable to 40, 30, or 10 percent? Our study does not presume an answer, choosing instead to estimate benchmarks for the delayed human cost of the Civil War's psychological traumas.

(2003), 229–252; Bernice Andrews et al., "Delayed-Onset Posttraumatic Stress Disorder: A Systematic Review of the Evidence," *American Journal of Psychiatry* 164 (2007), 1319–1326.

Benchmarks offer an additional approach to the question of significance. Readjusted veterans are one possible reference group in a study of ex-soldiers' psychological disorders, but civilians provide an equally meaningful comparison. Did Union veterans and their families, and civilians in general, experience mental illness and suicide at different rates and in different ways? Since these were recognized as important social problems, an answer offers insights about the Civil War's aftermath.

Chapters 4 and 5 trace the toll of these traumas through the initial postwar years and the remainder of the nineteenth century. Most of the findings in these and the preceding chapters apply to white veterans, though African Americans are included where evidence permits. Black veterans encountered trials of their own, however, and Chapter 6 examines the postwar struggles of the enlisted men who joined the US Colored Troops and their officers.

Drawing on a trove of statements by pension applicants transcribed as part of the Early Indicators project (see the appendix), we allow ex-soldiers to speak about their own conditions whenever possible. Much of this study's findings on suicide come from the exceptionally complete death records of Massachusetts. We return to the Bay State in Chapter 7 to compare past and present veterans' suicides. The comparison is a reminder that however alarming the current plight of veterans may be, we have passed this way before.

1

What Is a Union Veteran?

The choice of verb in this question is deliberate. Historians' conception of veterans differs from that of contemporaries. The late nineteenth-century definition comprised virtually all who had served in the US armed forces, but the focus in our time is more circumscribed. Drawn by drama and guided by availability of evidence, we concentrate on those whose lives were ruled by the irrepressible conflict.

Historians have acknowledged this fixation on war-ravaged veterans. Recognizing that those with severe problems were more likely to write about them, one author conceded that "the best-adjusted men at times fade from the narrative, and the less fortunate, marginalized men take center stage." To another historian, "all these dark elements describe the margins not the mainstream of Civil War experience," because most veterans readapted to civilian life.

Have we imposed on the past our preoccupation with the mental health of twenty-first-century veterans? If nearly all Civil War veterans resumed their former lives, the ordeals of the remainder would constitute a relative molehill. If evidence points instead to a broader maladjustment, veterans' physical and psychological afflictions would signify a genuine crisis of the past.[1]

If we are to weigh readjustment against veterans' hardships, we must first weigh the challenges of gauging either one. Numbers derived from the Civil War's destructiveness furnish one metric of hardship. More than one-fourth of Union survivors had been wounded. Approximately 25,000 Union soldiers survived with amputations. At least 15,000 Union soldiers had been classified by army physicians as "insane" or diagnosed with "nostalgia" or "sunstroke," conditions that are discussed in Chapter 5. More than 22,000 Union veterans, 90 percent of whom had health problems, lived in soldiers' homes in 1890. A decade later, more than 300,000 Union veterans were drawing federal pensions for war-related disabilities, plus another 400,000 for subsequent health problems. Studies of pension records

---

[1] James Marten, *Sing Not War: The Lives of Union and Confederate Veterans in Gilded Age America* (Chapel Hill: University of North Carolina Press, 2011), 3; Gary W. Gallagher quoted in Tony Horwitz, "The Civil War's Hidden Legacy," *Smithsonian*, January 2015, 46; see also Gary W. Gallagher and Kathryn S. Meier, "Coming to Terms with Civil War Military History," *Journal of the Civil War Era* 4 (2014): 487–508.

suggest that wartime traumas, especially high mortality and desertion rates among comrades, were associated with postwar psychological illness and early death. The estimate of "more than a million men [on both sides] whose bodies were torn and shattered" may be no exaggeration.[2]

---

[2] Larry M. Logue and Peter Blanck, *Race, Ethnicity, and Disability: Veterans and Benefits in Post–Civil War America* (New York: Cambridge University Press, 2010), 46–47 (29 percent of white survivors and 12 percent of African Americans had been hospitalized for a wound). For an estimate of surviving Union amputees, see Brian Matthew Jordan, *Marching Home: Union Veterans and Their Unending Civil War* (New York: Liveright, 2015), 255n. On insanity and other nervous disorders, see *Medical and Surgical History of the War of the Rebellion*, 6 vols. (Washington, DC: US Government Printing Office, 1870–1888), 1:639, 711; B. Christopher Frueh and Jeffrey A. Smith, "Suicide, Alcoholism, and Psychiatric Illness among Union Forces during the US Civil War," *Journal of Anxiety Disorders* 26 (2012): 769–775. On soldiers' home residents, see US Census Office, *Report on Population of the United States at the Eleventh Census* (Washington, DC: US Government Printing Office, 1897), Pt. II, clxxiv–clxxv (residents included those in state and federal homes). On pensioners, see William Henry Glasson, *Federal Military Pensions in the United States* (New York: Oxford University Press, 1918), 271. For studies using pension records, see Judith Pizarro, Roxane Cohen Silver, and JoAnn Prause, "Physical and Mental Health Costs of Traumatic War Experiences among Civil War Veterans," *Archives of General Psychiatry* 63 (2006): 193–200; Dora L. Costa and Matthew Kahn, "Health, Wartime Stress, and Unit Cohesion: Evidence from Union Army Veterans," *Demography* 47 (2010): 45–66. On the estimate of 1 million damaged men, see Megan Kate Nelson, *Ruin Nation: Destruction and the American Civil War* (Athens: University of Georgia Press, 2012), 161.

As stark as these figures are, they strike only glanc-ingly at the mountain-or-molehill question. On one hand, no one would deny the readaptation ordeal of James Forrest. A wound received in the Atlanta campaign led to amputation of Forrest's right leg. After a stay in a soldier's home, Forrest rejoined his wife and moved from Ohio to Nebraska in the early 1880s. He farmed and found work as a night watch-man, but his wound gave him no peace. A boarder reported that Forrest "would go out doors, lie down on the ground and cry, from his great suffering." Forrest ended his misery with a bullet to the chest in 1887.[3]

On the other hand, it is hard to discern a readjustment crisis in the career of former soldier Charles Champlin. A carpenter after the war, Champlin later joined the Water-town, New York, police force, working his way up from patrol-man to police chief. He was nonetheless awarded a pen-sion in 1891 for hearing loss, varicose veins, and various minor maladies. The presence of both men in the popula-tion of pensioners reminds us that aggregate figures cast an occluded light on the mainstream and dark edges of veter-ans' experience.[4]

---

[3] Affidavit of Herman Eades, May 28, 1889, Pension File of James A. Forrest, 21st Ohio Infantry, RG 15, National Archives; Record of James A. Forrest, Registers of Veterans at National Homes for Dis-abled Volunteer Soldiers, National Archives Microfilm Publication T1749, Genealogical Society of Utah.

[4] "Strong Men as Pensioners," *New York Times*, Mar. 30, 1894.

Approached from a different direction, however, aggregates may yet tell a tale. If we are questioning the absorption of veterans into the American population, we should make the larger comparisons that the question implies. Censuses registered the junctures of the life course, where readapted veterans should be indistinguishable from their peers. Three sources are available for a comparison. Manuscript schedules from a census of New York in 1865 provide information on Civil War veterans. A sample of more than 74,000 white and African American recruits, compiled for the Early Indicators of Later Work Levels, Disease, and Death project, includes information from military records, pension files, and federal census returns. The Minnesota Population Center has constructed samples of households for all extant federal censuses, allowing a profile of the larger American population.[5]

Union Veterans and Life Chances

Several states conducted censuses as the war was ending, and a federal count came five years later. Historians

[5] Census schedules from New York's 1865 census are available for 46 of 60 counties (New York City's schedules are among those missing); New York State Census, 1865, Genealogical Society of Utah. For information on the Early Indicators samples (hereafter cited as EI) and the Minnesota Population Center's Integrated Public Use Microdata Series (hereafter cited as IPUMS), see the appendix.

typically examine occupations in censuses to determine social mobility from one enumeration to the next, but veterans were worried about employment now. Though editorialists urged employers "to see that every situation at their disposal should be filled by men who have served their country" and a public official maintained that "the greater part [of Union veterans] quietly returned to the avocations of civil life with an industry in no degree impaired by their recent life in the field," other accounts were less sanguine. The *New York Times* reported that "thousands of discharged soldiers are now in this city seeking employment." Veterans besieged placement bureaus in New York and other cities, but employers seemed wary of returned combatants. "They are actually afraid to employ us," wrote one ex-soldier.[6]

Arriving in the midst of this employment crisis, census-takers in New York and Rhode Island conducted makeshift

---

[6] *New York Times*, May 7, 1865; Franklin B. Hough, *Census of the State of New York for 1865* (Albany, NY: Charles Van Benthuysen, 1867), 737; *New York Times*, June 16, 1865; Jordan, *Marching Home*, 54. See also Marten, *Sing Not War*, 55–59; Michael C. C. Adams, *Living Hell: The Dark Side of the Civil War* (Baltimore, MD: Johns Hopkins University Press, 2014), 192–193. For an overview of state censuses, see Ann S. Lainhart, *State Census Records* (Baltimore, MD: Genealogical Publishing, 1991). Studies of social mobility among veterans include Russell L. Johnson, "The Civil War Generation: Military Service and Mobility in Dubuque, Iowa, 1860–1870," *Journal of Social History* 32 (1999): 791–820; Lawrence A. Kreiser Jr., "A Socioeconomic Study of Veterans of the 103rd Ohio Volunteer Infantry Regiment after the Civil War," *Ohio History* 107 (1998): 171–184.

Table 1.1. *Selected characteristics of veterans sampled from 1865 New York census*

Median age	26
Percentage single	49
Percentage household head	42
Percentage relative of head	45
Percentage boarder or employee	12
Percentage reporting disability	25
Percentage with occupation left blank	14

surveys of Union veterans. New York's effort was especially ambitious: enumerators were directed to identify current and former soldiers and to follow up with particulars of each man's service and questions about disabilities. No one should harbor illusions about the accuracy of the outcome. The census's director confessed that the military information was "manifestly liable to error through want of information or otherwise." His successor pointed to other results that were "utterly worthless for statistical purposes." Flaws in these returns, however, are occasions to learn about veterans and their peers.[7]

Table 1.1 summarizes characteristics of Union veterans sampled from the 1865 New York census. The profile comports with civilians' anxieties about footloose ex-soldiers:

[7] Hough, *Census of New York*, 610; C. W. Seaton, *Census of the State of New York for 1875* (Albany, NY: Weed, Parsons, 1877), x. Rhode Island identified veterans in 1865, but without New York's detailed questions; see Lainhart, *Census Records,* 85–88, 99.

half were 25 or younger, nearly half were single, only two-fifths were heads of household, one in four claimed a disability, and one in seven had no reported occupation.[8]

But if young unemployed veterans posed a problem, their peers were worse. Census-takers had a mandate for recording all young men's presence or absence of an occupation. "The name of the business which the person is known and reputed to follow" was to be listed for every male over 15. "If a person follow [sic] no particular occupation, the space is to be filled with the word 'none.'" Enumerators usually complied when they interviewed household heads – only 5 percent had a blank occupation listing – but they treated dependents differently.[9]

Table 1.2 focuses on dependent sons (that is, those listed as "son" or "child" and reported as single), comparing

---

[8] The data summarized in Tables 1.1 and 1.2 are samples from manuscript schedules of the 1865 census of New York. Random pages were chosen from the extant schedules, and information was recorded for the veterans and dependent nonveterans who appeared on the pages; large urban areas were oversampled as partial compensation for New York City's absence. The total sample comprises 1,018 cases. Health queries for veterans included options for "Health good," "Health permanently impaired," loss of appendages, other wounds, and survival without wounds, plus a "Remarks" column. Table 1.1's entry for disabilities includes veterans with impaired health plus those with remarked-upon major wounds. On civilians' image of "corrupted" ex-soldiers, see Marten, *Sing Not War,* 45–54; Jordan, *Marching Home,* 41–44.

[9] *Instructions for Taking the Census of the State of New York* (Albany, NY: Weed, Parsons, 1865), 19–20.

Table 1.2. *Dependent relatives with blank occupation listings, veterans and nonveterans sampled from 1865 New York census*

	Percentage with occupation left blank
Veterans	18
Nonveterans	30

veterans to a sample of nonveterans from the same census. Census-takers ignored the occupations of a substantial number of dependent veterans, but they were almost twice as likely to neglect nonveterans, leaving a blank where an occupation (or "none") should have appeared. "None" appeared in fewer than 5 percent of these dependents' entries, suggesting that enumerators balked at the tedium of recording occupations for long lists of relatives.

Why would dependent veterans have been an exception? More veterans working would fly in the face of an employment crisis, except for two realities. An inquiry about residents' "profession, trade, or occupation" was not a query about their activities that day or week. Though people voiced distress about out-of-work veterans in 1865, unemployment had yet to acquire its modern meaning of a governmentally remediable social ill. Drawing on preindustrial conceptions, public policy viewed individuals as either productive or nonproductive. With no state priority at stake, census directors saw no need to inquire into workers' temporary inactivity. Even if census-takers had been diligent, there would have been nothing contradictory about an erstwhile clerk, for example, seeking any employment he could find until he regained his proper place.[10]

But enumerators were not diligent. Imprecision in classification was compounded by apparent capriciousness in identifying occupations at all. Yet Table 1.2 shows a pattern in the omissions, one that favored dependent veterans over their civilian peers. One clue hints at a reason for the pattern. Census-taker Ebenezer Stevens found 23 former soldiers in the town of Grafton in Rensselaer County. He left no blanks for their occupations; instead, he assigned 20 of them the occupation of "soldier." These men were no longer in the army, and many had had an occupation before the war.

We cannot know what Stevens was thinking, or even which of the census-listed Ebenezer Stevenses he was. We

---

[10] On evolving conceptions of unemployment, see Alexander Keyssar, *Out of Work: The First Century of Unemployment in Massachusetts* (New York: Cambridge University Press, 1986), 1–6; Margo A. Conk, "Occupational Classification in the United States Census: 1870–1940," *Journal of Interdisciplinary History* 9 (1978): 111–130. The director of the 1870 US census divided the male population into four groups: men with "gainful occupations"; students; men with "permanent bodily or mental infirmities"; and "the numbers of the criminal and pauper classes." Francis A. Walker, *The Statistics of the Population of the United States ... from the Original Returns of the Ninth Census* (Washington, DC: US Government Printing Office, 1872), 660.

do know that he made a sharp distinction between veterans and nonveterans, even if the occupational designation was wrong. Other enumerators were doing something similar, if not so obvious. In more readily assigning occupations to dependent veterans, census-takers acknowledged a contrast between ex-soldiers and their neighbors.

Poor Man's War?

Marriage, household headship, and a recognized occupation have stood as markers of maturity in most times and places. In assigning occupations to dependent veterans while ignoring nonveteran peers, enumerators conferred one of these symbols on the ex-soldiers. They may have flouted their orders, and their returns may have said little about veterans' actual plight, but census-takers' actions tacitly commended a distinctive veteran population in their midst.

But neighbors' admiration did not guarantee an income. When federal census-takers arrived in 1870, they brought the familiar concept of occupation-as-identity, and they made no attempt to identify veterans. Their returns, however, provide several advantages over the New York census. The Early Indicators samples of veterans (the EI samples) include connections to the 1870 census, and the Minnesota Population Center samples (the Integrated Public Use Microdata Samples [IPUMS]) offer a comparison with the general population. The size and scope of these samples also allow inclusion of African Americans. Moreover, the 1870 census contains a gauge of economic well-being that hints at veterans' reintegration.[11]

Census-takers were instructed to inquire about two forms of wealth. After requesting the value of any real estate residents owned, enumerators asked them about personal property, which meant anything else of value, except clothing. Fewer than 10 percent of black veterans claimed any real estate, so the more widespread personal property serves here as the measure of economic circumstances.[12]

If the employment crisis of 1865 had been short-lived, veterans should have regained enough wealth to be indistinguishable from their peers. Table 1.3 indicates, however, that neither whites nor African American veterans disappeared

---

[11] From contemporary indictments to more recent analyses, the 1870 census has long been the epitome of underenumeration. A reassessment, however, has estimated the 1870 undercount at 6 percent among northern-born white males, falling within the range of 4.2 to 7.8 percent for all pre-1940 censuses. J. David Hacker, "New Estimates of Census Coverage in the United States, 1850–1930," *Social Science History* 37 (2013): 71–101. See the appendix for details on the EI and IPUMS samples.

[12] No notation was to be made when personal property was valued at less than $100. Enumerator instructions reproduced in US Census Bureau, *Measuring America: The Decennial Censuses from 1790 to 2000* (Washington, DC: US Census Bureau, 2002), 15. For an analysis of the federal censuses' wealth data that finds some discrepancies but general agreement with tax rolls, see Richard H. Steckel, "Census Manuscript Schedules Matched with Property Tax Lists," *Historical Methods* 27 (1994): 71–86.

Table 1.3. *Average personal property in 1870, EI samples of veterans and IPUMS sample of men age 20–59*

	Average value of personal property ($)
White veterans	588
All white men 20–59	713
African American veterans	70
All African American men 20–59	45

Note: Averages adjusted to compensate for differing age distributions. Whites in IPUMS sample restricted to selected states; see note 13.

into the general population. White veterans were considerably poorer than white men overall, but the difference may have had little to do with the war. Though the contemporary indictment of a "poor man's war" was an oversimplification, studies of participation have frequently found that Union recruits were less wealthy than their noncombatant peers.[13]

[13] Linkage of the sample of white veterans to the 1870 census by EI researchers is ongoing. Those linked so far lived predominantly in Delaware, Iowa, Illinois, Indiana, Kansas, Maine, Michigan, Minnesota, Missouri, Ohio, West Virginia, and Wisconsin. For comparability, whites shown from IPUMS samples in Table 1.3 are also restricted to those states. The EI samples present another challenge, since pension information was the main source used to connect veterans to the census, creating a bias against those who did not apply for aid; a few nonapplicants were nonetheless linked, and they are weighted in this analysis to mitigate the bias. The age distribution of veterans and nonveterans differed substantially, and each comparison in Tables 1.3 and 1.4 is adjusted to compensate for the difference. Studies that find disproportionate Union army

The finding is affirmed by another comparison of the EI and IPUMS data. Table 1.4 shows that, when the veterans

---

enlistment among poorer men include Johnson, "Civil War Generation"; Wayne K. Durrill, *War of Another Kind: A Southern Community in the Great Rebellion* (New York: Oxford University Press, 1990), 229–242; W. J. Rorabaugh, "Who Fought for the North in the Civil War? Concord, Massachusetts, Enlistments," *Journal of American History* 73 (1986): 695–701; Susan S. Rugh, "'Awful Calamities Now upon Us': The Civil War in Fountain Green, Illinois," *Journal of the Illinois State Historical Society* 93 (2000): 9–42; Kathleen Shaw, "'Johnny Has Gone for a Soldier': Youth Enlistment in a Northern County," *Pennsylvania Magazine of History and Biography* 135 (2011): 419–446; Mark A. Snell, "'If They Would Know What I Know It Would Be Pretty Hard to Raise One Company in York': Recruiting, the Draft, and Society's Response in York County, Pennsylvania, 1861–1865," in Paul A. Cimbala and Randall M. Miller, eds., *Union Soldiers and the Northern Home Front: Wartime Experiences, Postwar Adjustments* (New York: Fordham University Press, 2002), 69–116. Mixed results on wealth and enlistment appear in Steven J. Buck, "'A Contest in Which Blood Must Flow Like Water': Du Page County and the Civil War," *Illinois Historical Journal* 87 (1994): 2–20; Maris A. Vinovskis, "Have Social Historians Lost the Civil War? Some Preliminary Demographic Speculations," in Maris A. Vinovskis, ed., *Toward a Social History of the American Civil War: Exploratory Essays* (New York: Cambridge University Press, 1990), 1–30; Thomas R. Kemp, "Community and War: The Experience of Two New Hampshire Towns," in Maris A. Vinovskis, ed., *Toward a Social History of the American Civil War: Exploratory Essays* (New York: Cambridge University Press, 1990), 31–77. Most of the latter studies assign fathers' wealth to dependent sons, raising the apparent wealth of young soldiers because they enlisted in disproportionate numbers. The present study makes no assumptions about the wealth of dependents, treating enlistees and civilians alike by adjusting for age distribution differences.

Table 1.4. *Average personal property in 1860, EI samples of men who enlisted and IPUMS sample of white men age 15–59*

	Average value of personal property ($)
Whites who later enlisted	119
All white men 15–59	223

Note: Averages adjusted to compensate for differing age distributions.

examined in Table 1.3 are traced back to the 1860 census, their personal wealth likewise fell short of that owned by the aggregate white population. The tendency of poorer men to enlist did not render them less distinctive after the war; it suggests that they were a distinctive postwar population because they had been distinctive beforehand.

African American veterans stood out in the opposite direction. They had acquired more wealth by 1870 than had black men in general. Their relative prosperity accords with studies that point to veterans' economic gains and political leadership in black communities. At the same time, Table 1.4 accentuates the modest nature of the gains. Black soldiers may have had wider experience than civilians during the war and qualified for back pay and bounties afterward, but their average personal property was barely one-eighth of that held by white veterans.[14]

[14] See Joseph Glatthaar, *Forged in Battle: The Civil War Alliance of Black Soldiers and White Officers* (New York: Free Press, 1990), 236–238; Donald R. Shaffer, *After the Glory: The Struggles of Black Civil War Veterans* (Lawrence: University Press of Kansas, 2004),

Disability and Life Chances

These comparisons show that Union veterans differed from their neighbors in ways that have meaning for us, but they also underscore the importance of contemporary meanings. Race mattered, and experience in the war conferred on African Americans an economic benefit that it did not, on the whole, grant to whites. Disabilities mattered too, but their nature and effects call for a different approach. Identifying veterans "with disabilities" requires choosing among flawed alternatives. The records of ex-soldiers in the EI samples are full of army physicians' diagnoses, but the terminology is sometimes alien ("phrenitis" and "hydrothosis," for example), and vague ("general debility" or "wound in side").

Federal pensions, predicated before 1890 on war-related maladies, were alternative markers of disability. They depended, however, on veterans' willingness to apply, which was in turn influenced by race, ethnicity, changes in pension laws, and local politics. On the other hand, a veteran's having been discharged from the army on a surgeon's certification is a consistent identifier of disability (Figure 1.1).

53–59; Richard Reid, "USCT Veterans in Post–Civil War North Carolina," in John David Smith, ed., *Black Soldiers in Blue: African American Troops in the Civil War Era* (Chapel Hill: University of North Carolina Press, 2002), 391–422. Pension income raised African American veterans' wealth. Table 1.3, however, shows that pensions did not bring white veterans to parity with civilians, partly because fewer black ex-soldiers than whites were receiving Union army pensions in 1870.

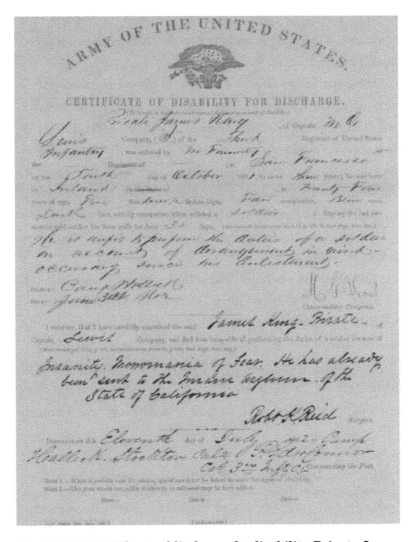

Figure 1.1. A certificate of discharge for disability. Private James King was "incapable of performing the duties of a soldier" due to "monomania." Civil War Compiled Service Records, Record Group 94, National Archives

Approximately 16 percent of white war survivors and 8 percent of African Americans in the EI samples received disability discharges.[15]

Disabilities are barely discernible in veterans' economic well-being. Both white and African American men with medical discharges had personal wealth within a few dollars of the veterans' averages reported in Table 1.3. To be sure, averages obscure the predicament of men such as James Forrest, whose disability precluded most ways of earning a conventional living. Forrest's financial hardship was lessened by a federal pension that began at $8 a month in 1865 and rose to $30 by 1883.

That Forrest's pension did little for his physical anguish prompts us to look elsewhere for disabilities' consequences. Mortality is the touchstone for these consequences, and can be estimated for veterans and the larger population. It is not clear what we should expect from death rates of veterans with disabilities. They returned home with serious health impairments, but they had survived wounds,

[15] On factors influencing veterans' likelihood of applying for a pension, including the activities of claim agents, see Logue and Blanck, *Race, Ethnicity*, 48–54, 92–97, 111–127. On procedures for disability discharges, see Roberts Bartholow, *A Manual of Instructions for Enlisting and Discharging Soldiers* (Philadelphia: Lippincott, 1864). Medical discharges are imperfect indicators of disability, because men occasionally reenlisted after receiving them; see Eric T. Dean Jr., *Shook over Hell: Post-Traumatic Stress, Vietnam, and the Civil War* (Cambridge, MA: Harvard University Press, 1997), 88–89.

injuries, and diseases and had cheated the ravages of an overburdened hospital system. Did this endurance produce a "survivor effect" that would have lowered the mortality of veterans with disabilities?[16]

Table 1.5 indicates that it generally did not. The table shows death probabilities for the 1870s and the 1890s: that is, given the mortality rates for each group, how many men in a thousand who reached age 30, 40, and so on would die in the decade? The comparison for white men classifies them as veterans with and without a disability discharge, versus an estimate for all whites in the same decades. The number of African Americans in the EI samples is smaller, so black veterans are analyzed regardless of disability and compared to an estimate for black men in 1900. Each comparison uses the three largest age groups of veterans.[17]

---

[16] For graphic descriptions of the risks of the Civil War, especially hospitalization, to life and limb, see Adams, *Living Hell*, 84–107; Nelson, *Ruin Nation*, 160–189; Kathryn S. Meier, *Nature's Civil War: Common Soldiers and the Environment in 1862 Virginia* (Chapel Hill: University of North Carolina Press, 2013), 65–98. For speculations about a survivor effect among those involved in various conflicts, see David Roelfs et al., "War-Related Stress and Mortality: A Meta-Analysis," *International Journal of Epidemiology* 39 (2010), 1507. See also John S. Billings, "The Health of the Survivors of the War," *Forum* 12 (1891–92), 652–658.

[17] Veterans' information is weighted in the same way as in Tables 1.3 and 1.4 to compensate for the disproportionately small number of nonpensioners. Probabilities in Table 1.5 correspond to $_{10}q_x$ values in a life table, that is, the probability of dying in the next 10 years after reaching a given age. Probabilities for US whites calculated

Table 1.5. *Deaths after reaching selected ages per 1,000 veterans in EI samples compared with estimates for US population, 1870–1879 and 1890–1899*

Age	White veterans without disability	White veterans with disability	US white men	African American veterans	US black men, 1900
1870–1879					
30	89	102	94	166	–
40	140	209	122	164	–
50	210	263	192	222	–
1890–1899					
50	153	155	171	254	247
60	293	324	323	373	419
70	505	615	588	553	687

Mortality for white veterans without disability discharges was similar to that of the overall population. In this respect, most veterans receded into ordinary life. Those with disabilities, however, carried a discernible burden. They ran a higher risk of death in the 1870s than did their peers, a risk that accelerated with age. Since many of the most vulnerable veterans had died early, their successors'

---

from q_x estimates in J. David Hacker, "Decennial Life Tables for the White Population of the United States, 1790–1900," *Historical Methods* 43 (2010), 45–79; probabilities for African Americans calculated from Michael R. Haines, "Estimated Life Tables for the United States, 1850–1910," *Historical Methods* 31 (1998), 149–169.

disadvantage dropped at the century's end, but their mortality again worsened faster with age than it did for other veterans.

In keeping with the wealth comparison shown earlier, black veterans' mortality was less severe than the 1900 estimate for all black men. Nonetheless, African American mortality provides a kind of worst-case perspective on the nineteenth-century risk of death. At most ages in both periods, African American veterans' and aggregate probability of dying exceeded the risk for whites.

Kaleidoscope of Circumstances

Like personal wealth, mortality is a coarse instrument, but both provide pieces of an answer to this chapter's opening question. They point only to *an* answer, not *the* answer, because aggregate measures register only tendencies. People unquestionably *have* tendencies, but few would argue that they *are* their tendencies. Nonetheless, those who refer to margins and mainstream of veterans' experience are making aggregate claims, leaving us to sort out which is which.

The comparisons shown here reveal no fixed boundaries between mainstream and margins. Young veterans received differential treatment from state census-takers, while household heads did not. Whether they had a disability or not, white veterans lagged behind the broader population in wealth, while black veterans inched ahead. White veterans without disabilities could expect to live as long as their peers, while white veterans with service-ending disabilities and African Americans died younger. If evocations of mainstream and margins imply a riverine analogy, veterans' actual circumstances might better be likened to a kaleidoscope of shifting individuals and circumstances.

America in the 1860s had likewise been a kaleidoscope, a jumble of people and institutions and economies. Yet no one would deny that one event unified the decade. It will not do to point out that only a minority of northern men joined the Union army. This is too cramped a view; the Civil War touched nearly everyone's life.[18]

So it was with veterans. James Forrest's fate was uncommon, but the shortened lives of veterans with disabilities point to broader influences governing their life course. Attending to the compulsions that drew Forrest to the barn with his revolver, and kept the war alive for other veterans, illuminates these influences. There was no "Union veteran" who epitomized the experience of more than a million former soldiers. There is, we will argue, evidence from ex-soldiers under stress that attests to forces, some rooted in their era and some timeless, that molded lives long after Appomattox.

[18] On northern participation, see Vinovskis, "Social Historians," 9.

2

Changed Men

We return to verbs. Union veterans reentered civilian society, but to conclude that they fully reintegrated is a sanguine assumption about men who stood out in ways described in the previous chapter. But the common verb of the era is at least as important as our contrived ones. Time and again, friends and relatives marveled at how returning veterans had changed. When Elisha Ellis came back to Wisconsin in 1865, his brother-in-law "noticed that his mind had changed." To a friend in Illinois, John Early "was a different man" on his return. Harrison Horr's former comrade saw "a marked change in his appearance" at a regimental reunion. Michael Hogan's neighbors reported that Hogan "was not himself so far as his mind was concerned" after his release from Andersonville Prison.[1]

This testimony was likely tailored to influence pension officials. No pension was at stake, however, when William Hensley's wife "stared at me like she was scared...because I looked so different," when a newspaper warned that a veteran's friends may "know him not, at once, for the change which has come over him," and when George Murray recalled that he "returned home a mere wreck of my former self."[2]

The four veterans of the opening paragraph are distinctive, however, for the lingering consequences of their changes. John Early was declared legally insane and placed under the care of his son. Michael Hogan was sent to a New York state insane asylum. Elisha Ellis and Harrison Horr committed suicide in the 1870s. Sequels such as these

[1] Deposition of Henry C. Fuller, Jan. 16, 1891, Pension File of Elisha W. Ellis, 23rd Wisconsin Infantry, RG 15, National Archives; Affidavit of Samuel Blair, Pension File of John M. Early, 59th Illinois Infantry, RG 15, National Archives; Marshall M. Clothier to Commissioner of Pensions, Pension File of Harrison Z. Horr, 31st Massachusetts Infantry, RG 15, National Archives; Affidavit of Elwood H. Pixley and Maria Pixley, June 25, 1889, Pension File of Michael J. Hogan, 100th New York Infantry, RG 15, National Archives.

[2] Hensley quoted in Brian Matthew Jordan, *Marching Home: Union Veterans and Their Unending Civil War* (New York: Liveright, 2015), 51; Newark [NJ] *Daily Advertiser*, June 21, 1865; George W. Murray, *A History of George W. Murray and His Long Confinement in Andersonville, Ga.* (Northampton, MA: Trumbull and Gere, n.d.), 29.

provide the bridge between aggregate indicators and individual experience.

Concentrating on ex-soldiers with the severest problems educes the objection discussed in the previous chapter. Institutional commitments and suicides were proportionally rare among veterans of the Civil War. This contention is true enough on its face, but a full response calls for an excursion into the epistemology of mental illness in the past.

As with assertions about mainstream and margins, insistence on the rarity of institutionalization and suicide rests on a faith in quantifiable boundaries. A population can be divided into those with disabilities and those without, asylum inmates and noninmates, or suicides and nonsuicides. Citing the divisions, skeptics reiterate the argument that the majority of people in a given circumstance had no disability, did not commit suicide, and did not enter an insane asylum. No one will disagree so long as the claim remains vague, but scholars prefer specificity. When suicide's incidence arises as a topic, it should become clear that the parameters of majority and minority are to be investigated rather than assumed.

Suicide in the "Inquiring Age"

A key obstacle impedes authoritative pronouncements on the incidence of suicide. Analysts typically rely on official suicide reports, but their utility has come under attack. The sociologist Jack Douglas made the most influential assault on the credibility of suicide statistics, concluding that they are "so greatly in error that they cannot be used for the scientific study of suicide." Douglas's indictment rests on two cornerstones. Official records are allegedly invalid: they register not total suicides but some lesser number resulting from imprecise definitions of suicide and intentional alteration to placate victims' relatives. The records are also unreliable: rather than variations in suicidal behavior, they register vagaries in official misclassification from place to place and time to time. Any study that intends to explore the occurrence of suicide must evaluate its evidence in light of these allegations.[3]

The death records of Massachusetts, which pioneered the collection of vital statistics in America, are the chief source for this book's investigation of suicides. We are keenly

---

[3] Jack D. Douglas, *The Social Meanings of Suicide* (Princeton, NJ: Princeton University Press, 1967), 230. For examples of Douglas's influence on historians, see Richard Bell, *We Shall Be No More: Suicide and Self-Government in the Newly United States* (Cambridge, MA: Harvard University Press, 2012), 277–278n; John C. Weaver, *Sadly Troubled History: The Meanings of Suicide in the Modern Age* (Montreal: McGill-Queen's Press, 2009), 47–51; Róisín Healy, "Suicide in Early Modern and Modern Europe," *Historical Journal* 49 (2006), 906; Victor Bailey, *"This Rash Act": Suicide across the Life Cycle in the Victorian City* (Stanford, CA: Stanford University Press, 1998), 37–84; Michael MacDonald and Terence R. Murphy, *Sleepless Souls: Suicide in Early Modern England* (New York: Oxford University Press, 1993), 3–4; Olive Anderson, *Suicide in Victorian and Edwardian England* (New York: Oxford University Press, 1987), 13–15.

aware of the criticism that attaches to studies of one place, even one so populous (Massachusetts was the seventh-largest state in 1880) and heterogeneous (there were roughly equal numbers of male textile workers and farmers, and one-third of the labor force were immigrants). No state was "typical" of America in the Gilded Age, but Massachusetts displays its suitability in another way. In the Early Indicators samples described in the previous chapter, 3.6 percent of Union veterans in Massachusetts died by suicide, compared to fewer than 1 percent of those living elsewhere. It strains credulity to suppose that the suicide rate in Massachusetts was more than three times that of the rest of the nation. The Bay State's atypicality lies chiefly in its inauguration of systematized record-keeping.[4]

Prompted by similar laws in England and elsewhere in Europe, Massachusetts legislators mandated in 1842 a uniform registration system for births, marriages, and deaths. Town clerks were required to record the particulars of each vital event on standard forms sent yearly to state officials. Massachusetts leaders declared that in "the inquiring age in which we live" they had "taken the lead" in adopting record-keeping "worthy of the state that has instituted [it]," but

---

[4] Massachusetts textile industries employed 44,773 male workers in 1880, and 39,148 men were farmers; 33.6 percent of the total labor force (that is; residents of both sexes over age 10) were born outside the United States. US Census Office, *Statistics of the Population of the United States at the Tenth Census* (Washington, DC: Government Printing Office, 1883), 828.

local residents were initially unimpressed. "The inhabitants do not," according to one clerk, "give themselves the least trouble in regard to furnishing the clerk with the necessary information," and Boston did not participate at all until 1849. As the legislature tightened reporting mandates and raised clerks' fees, however, death registration improved. A thorough analysis of Massachusetts's registration system estimated that 92 percent of deaths were being reported in 1860, rising to 98 percent by 1870.[5]

Many of the unrecorded deaths were private burials, undoubtedly including some suicides. And nonreporting was only one source of lost suicides. Uncertainty about drownings or railroad deaths could result in erroneous reports, as could connivance with decedents' families. Coroners, whose function was to rectify uncertainty and connivance, were

---

[5] Robert Gutman, "Birth and Death Registration in Massachusetts, II: The Inauguration of a Modern System, 1800–1849," *Milbank Memorial Fund Quarterly* 36 (1958), 373–402; *Registry and Returns of Births, Marriages and Deaths Occurring in the Commonwealth* (Boston: Dutton and Wentworth, 1851), viii, vii; *Annual Report to the Legislature Relating to the Registry and Returns of Births, Marriages and Deaths in Massachusetts* (Boston: Dutton and Wentworth, 1845), 16; Robert Gutman, "Birth and Death Registration in Massachusetts, III: The System Achieves a Form, 1849–1869," *Milbank Memorial Fund Quarterly* 37 (1959), 309–326; Robert Gutman, "The Accuracy of Vital Statistics in Massachusetts, 1842–1901" (PhD diss., Columbia University, 1956), 231. Massachusetts published registration reports hereafter cited as *Annual Reports of Vital Statistics*.

not obligated to report their findings to Massachusetts officials.

Nor were coroners' findings particularly trustworthy. Bay State physicians waged a protracted struggle against coroners, portraying them as "individuals entirely unacquainted with medical science ... [who] cannot be competent to determine the questions entrusted to them." The campaign succeeded in 1877, when the legislature became the first to eliminate the office altogether. Coroners, 43 of whom had served Boston alone, were replaced by two medical examiners in Boston and 73 elsewhere. From 1885 onward the state published medical examiners' summary findings along with mortality statistics compiled from the town clerks, providing a valuable gauge of suicide reporting.[6]

Figure 2.1 shows Massachusetts suicides per 100,000 white men from 1865 to 1900, comparing published clerks' reports with medical examiners' figures after 1885. Medical examiners began to find more suicides, revealing an anomaly in local registration. Prevailing suspicions about suicide records have taught us to expect a scattering of

[6] Jeffrey M. Jentzen, *Death Investigation in America: Coroners, Medical Examiners, and the Pursuit of Medical Certainty* (Cambridge, MA: Harvard University Press, 2009), 19. See also James C. Mohr, *Doctors and the Law: Medical Jurisprudence in Nineteenth-Century America* (Baltimore: Johns Hopkins University Press, 1996), 213–224.

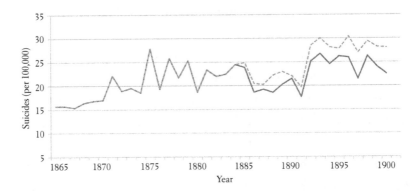

Figure 2.1. Massachusetts suicides per 100,000 men, from town clerks' reports, 1860–1900 (solid line); Massachusetts suicides per 100,000 men, from medical examiners' reports, 1885–1900 (broken line)

misclassifications, corresponding to local functionaries' varied competence. Yet Table 2.1, comparing Massachusetts counties' total suicides from the two sources, shows instead a bifurcation of omissions. All but 2 of the 14 counties misclassified a modest proportion of their suicides, for an

Table 2.1. *Massachusetts suicides reported by town clerks and medical examiners, and difference, 1885–1900*

Counties	Suicides reported by clerks	Suicides reported by MEs	Percentage ME increase
Bristol and Hampden	339	473	40.0
Rest of Massachusetts	3,136	3,478	10.9

average of 11 percent. Hampden county in western Massachusetts and Bristol in the southeast were stark outliers: misreporting there averaged two-fifths of suicides, nearly four times the average elsewhere.[7]

Another appraisal uses a different approach to gauge omitted suicides. Journalists had every incentive to ferret out self-destruction. When the nature of the act was beyond

---

[7] Numerators for rates in Figure 2.1 from *Annual Reports of Vital Statistics*. Denominators from Massachusetts Secretary of the Commonwealth, *Abstract of the Census of Massachusetts, from the Eighth US Census* (Boston: Wright and Potter, 1863), 59–61; Massachusetts Secretary of the Commonwealth, *Abstract of the Census of Massachusetts, 1865* (Boston: Wright and Potter, 1867), 2–3; US Census Office, *Ninth Census – Volume II: Vital Statistics of the United States* (Washington, DC: Government Printing Office, 1872), 565–574; Massachusetts Bureau of Statistics of Labor, *Census of Massachusetts: 1875,* 4 vols. (Boston: Albert J. Wright, 1876), I: 269; US Census Office, *Statistics of the Population of the United States at the Tenth Census* (Washington, DC: Government Printing Office, 1881), 592–593; Massachusetts Bureau of Statistics of Labor, *Census of Massachusetts: 1885,* 3 vols. (Boston: Wright and Potter, 1887), I: 434–435; US Census Office, *Report on the Population of the United States at the Eleventh Census* (Washington, DC: Government Printing Office, 1897), pt. II, 44–45; Massachusetts Bureau of Statistics of Labor, *Census of the Commonwealth of Massachusetts: 1895,* 7 vols. (Boston: Wright and Potter, 1896), II: 515; US Census Office, *Twelfth Census of the United States: Population* (Washington, DC: Government Printing Office, 1902), pt. II, 50–51. Population by age groups in noncensus years is estimated by interpolation. Since the *Annual Reports of Vital Statistics* published suicide numbers by age and sex *or* county, but not both, numbers by county in Table 2.1 reflect total suicides rather than those of men.

question, they explicated it to their audience, as when the "dissipated" Frank Porter "ended his wretched life by cutting his throat." And they took particular gratification from exposing attempts at concealment. When Asa Jones slashed his throat in 1865, a Worcester paper pointed out that "the facts were in our possession almost immediately after the occurrence, but were withheld by request; but as the matter is made public in the Boston papers, silence is no longer necessary." Newspapers' doggedness has made them an ideal check on other sources for elusive phenomena such as homicides and lynchings. Using an ingenious technique known as "capture–recapture," comparing sources can likewise point to undetected suicides.[8]

The years 1865 and 1875 are good candidates for an estimate of missing suicides in Massachusetts. According to Figure 2.1, 1865 was a year of few suicides, while 1875 was a peak year and was midway to the advent of medical examiners' published statistics. When subjected to the capture–recapture test, which weighs duplications against suicides appearing in only one source, either or both years might

[8] *Beverly Citizen*, April 18, 1891; [Worcester] *Massachusetts Spy*, Nov. 24, 1865. For a discussion of capture–recapture's utility in evaluating homicide reports, see Douglas Lee Eckberg, "Stalking the Elusive Homicide: A Capture–Recapture Approach to the Estimation of Post-Reconstruction South Carolina Killings," *Social Science History* 25 (2001), 67–91; for its application to lynching, see Michael A. Trotti, "What Counts: Trends in Racial Violence in the Postbellum South," *Journal of American History* 100 (2013), 383–384.

reveal substantial misclassification through negligence or oversight. Yet the test actually suggests that only four suicides (or 6 percent) were missing in 1865 and three (or 2 percent) were overlooked in 1875.[9]

Though the comparisons indicate that some suicides were omitted through oversight or collusion, they offer two reassurances about the utility of the suicide statistics. Except for Hampden and Bristol counties, both estimates of misclassifications fall at the low end of the 10 to 50 percent omissions range posited by Jack Douglas. Moreover, the trend in clerk-reported suicides shown in Figure 2.1 closely follows peaks and valleys in the medical examiners' findings.

It thus appears justifiable to use published statistics, adjusted for their most obvious flaws, as the entry point

---

[9] Comparing death registration with newspaper reports requires names and other information for individual suicides, which are not included in the summary reports cited above. The evaluation therefore uses manuscript ledgers kept by town clerks, recording information transcribed from death certificates (Massachusetts Registration of Deaths, 1841–1915, Genealogical Society of Utah); a separate search was conducted in Massachusetts newspapers. As applied to Massachusetts in 1865, capture–recapture uses the number of male suicides that appear only in official registration returns (27) multiplied by the number that appear only in newspapers (5) divided by the number that appear in both places (37); the result is an estimated 3.6 undetected suicides. For 1875, the number of suicides in official returns only was 26, and the number in newspapers only was 12. Dividing the product of these numbers by 103, the number appearing in both sources, produces an estimate of 3 undetected suicides.

Figure 2.2. Massachusetts death register for 1898, recording former Pvt. Richard G. Lillie's suicide by gunshot on April 25. Lillie's adversities are discussed in Chapter 4. Massachusetts Registration of Deaths, 1841–1915, Genealogical Society of Utah

for a fuller exploration of suicide among veterans and civilians in late nineteenth-century Massachusetts (Figure 2.2). Figure 2.3 is a modified charting of the state's suicide rate for white men, excluding Bristol and Hampden counties

Figure 2.3. Modified Massachusetts suicides per 100,000 white men

through 1885 and using medical examiners' reports for all counties afterward.[10]

Suicide and Psychological Forces

No matter how trustworthy, suicide records cannot refute the aforementioned contention that most people, no matter what their circumstances, do not take their own lives. Even when the population "at risk" is restricted to those with a realistic possibility of dying by suicide – white men over age 20 – fewer than 30 men per 100,000 committed suicide in Massachusetts in the late nineteenth century.

But to leave the issue there is disingenuous. A categorical distinction between suicides and nonsuicides ignores the Indiana veteran Richard Ketchum, whose wartime injury drove him "towards melancholia" and made him "almost suicidal," but who died of natural causes 15 years later. It misjudges Alfred Leeper, who wrote in 1904 that he had "suffered all the agonies of hell" and attempted suicide four times, but who survived until 1916 (Figure 2.4). Suicides may have been rare, but they produced evidence that

[10] Jack Douglas avers that reforms in collecting suicide statistics "have always led to increases in the suicide rates." We must therefore "assume that [rates before reforms] underestimate the 'potential suicide rates' by anywhere from 10% to 50%"; Douglas, *Social Meanings*, 195. To allow for a changing age structure, rates in Figure 2.2 have been adjusted to correspond to Massachusetts's age distribution as it stood in 1860.

Figure 2.4. Former Sgt. Alfred Leeper of the 115th Illinois Infantry, about 1900. Decades after serving in the Western theater, Leeper was institutionalized for insanity. From Isaac H. C. Royse, *History of the 115th Regiment, Illinois Volunteer Infantry*

can illuminate the plight of a much larger population in extremis.[11]

11 Surgeon's Certificate, Dec. 30, 1889, Pension File of Richard R. Ketchum, 146th Indiana Infantry, RG 15, National Archives; Alfred Leeper to Commissioner of Pensions, April 20, 1904, Pension File of Alfred B. Leeper, 115th Illinois Infantry, ibid. Leeper's cause of death is undocumented.

This illumination is the goal of our book. Even if it were possible, explaining suicide itself is beyond our purpose. Suicide is a hydra-headed problem that has frustrated several disciplines. Psychologists, sociologists, and medical researchers have long vied for the true key to self-murder, only to find competitors insisting that each discipline leaves more unexplained than explained. Ours is a more diffident approach. We are not offended by the untidiness of multiple interested parties attaching various meanings to the act of suicide. We have gathered evidence of suicidal thoughts and actions from veterans, family members, journalists, and public officials, deepening our exploration of the psychological forces unleashed by America's deadliest war.[12]

---

[12] See the description of competition for suicide's key in Howard I. Kushner, *Self-Destruction in the Promised Land: A Psychocultural Biology of American Suicide* (New Brunswick, NJ: Rutgers University Press, 1989), 62–90.

3

When War Came

This book is primarily about the Civil War's delayed casualties. Yet wars also shape the psychological landscape while they are under way. To survey one such landscape, we begin with Massachusetts on the eve of the war, and with the efforts of early social scientists to explain suicide.

Having pondered statistics on suicide, several nineteenth-century scholars announced the discovery of its central dynamic. The advent of modern society, signified by the rise of industrial production and the growth of cities, had disrupted the affective and kinship bonds that normally deterred suicide. It was little wonder that suicide rates rose along with economic development, and that they were highest in the largest cities.[1]

[1] Howard I. Kushner, "Suicide, Gender, and the Fear of Modernity in Nineteenth-Century Medical and Social Thought," *Journal of Social*

This is a sweeping theory resting heavily on supposition, and it has met criticism from several perspectives. Yet it remains influential, forming a backdrop for considering Massachusetts in 1860. The Bay State was an exemplar of the developments associated with modernization. Internal migration and famine-induced Irish immigration had doubled Boston's population since 1840, and the state's industrial production had risen nearly 70 percent since 1850.[2]

And suicides were indeed common in Massachusetts. Local records and newspaper reports for 1860 identify 89 Massachusetts men who died by suicide, or 26 per 100,000.

History 26 (1993), 461–490, gives a useful account of the rise of this theory.

[2] For critiques of the theory's applicability, see Olive Anderson, "Did Suicide Increase with Industrialization in Victorian England?" *Past and Present* 86 (1980), 149–173; Jack D. Douglas, *The Social Meanings of Suicide* (Princeton, NJ: Princeton University Press, 1967), 225–227. For a mixed assessment that demonstrates the theory's continuing influence, see Steven Stack, "Suicide: A 15-Year Review of the Sociological Literature – Part II: Modernization and the Social Integration Perspectives," *Suicide and Life-Threatening Behavior* 30 (2000), 163–176. For a more nuanced use of the thesis, see Roger Lane, *Violent Death in the City: Suicide, Accident, and Murder in Nineteenth-Century Philadelphia* (Cambridge, MA: Harvard University Press, 1979). Comparable industrial production figures are unavailable for 1840, so totals cited here begin in 1850. In that year, Massachusetts industries' total product was valued at $151,137,145, and the value rose by 69 percent to $255,545,922 in 1860; J. D. B. DeBow, *Compendium of the Seventh Census* (Washington, DC: Beverly Tucker, 1854), 179; US Census Bureau, *Manufactures of the United States in 1860* (Washington, DC: Government Printing Office, 1865), 257.

By comparison, the Bay State's rate in 2014 was 18 suicides per 100,000 men. Boston, whose size and growth exemplified the urban maelstrom described by suicide researchers, failed to support their theory. The city's suicide rate was, like that of the rest of the state, 26 per 100,000 men.[3]

Visible Acts

If the actual frequency of suicide in 1860 was somewhat higher than today's rate, the cultural immediacy of the act was beyond compare. Ours is an age of sharply demarcated public and private spheres. Some individuals, especially politicians, entertainers, and athletes, are public figures whose lives are open to limitless intrusions. When a celebrity dies by his or her own hand, a debate typically ensues about the intractability of suicide. Everyone else presumes the privilege of choosing which personal information will be disseminated. Only in extraordinary

---

[3] Suicides in 1860 gleaned from town clerks' manuscript ledgers (Massachusetts Registration of Deaths, 1841–1915, Genealogical Society of Utah; hereafter cited as Massachusetts Deaths) and from Massachusetts newspapers. Six additional men under age 20 died by suicide, for a teenage suicide rate of 11 per 100,000. Suicide rate for 2014 obtained from Centers for Disease Control and Prevention, National Violent Death Reporting System, www.cdc.gov/injury/wisqars/nvdrs.html (since all Massachusetts suicides in 1860 were whites, the 2014 comparison uses white men over age 20). Massachusetts had quite different age distributions in the two periods; adjusting the 1860 suicide rate to compensate for the different distributions raises it to 35 per 100,000 men.

circumstances, such as when they seek to publicize deaths among veterans, do families waive their right to privacy about suicide.[4]

The visibility of suicide in nineteenth-century communities could hardly be more alien to our privacy-based worldview. Where we see the need to maintain boundaries, people of the nineteenth century assumed a seamless web of face-to-face familiarity. Urbanization in places such as Massachusetts eroded this intimacy, but journalists were glad to serve as proxies for traditional conversation and gossip. They filled the columns of the penny press with "local intelligence," and as we noted in the previous chapter, they were especially diligent in probing suicides.[5]

A few self-murders were undeniably newsworthy. William Holden walked to a spot near the flagpole on Boston Common and shot himself through the heart, whereupon "a large crowd surrounded the body, like a flock of vultures, all

[4] See, e.g., Howard Somers and Jean Somers, "On Losing a Veteran Son to a Broken System," *New York Times*, Nov. 11, 2013; Yochi Dreazen, *The Invisible Front: Love and Loss in an Era of Endless War* (New York: Crown, 2014); Dave Phillipps, "A Unit Stalked by Suicide, Trying to Save Itself," *New York Times,* Sept. 20, 2015.

[5] On the disjunction between modern and traditional notions of public and private, see Michael Zuckerman, "The Irrelevant Revolution: 1776 and Since," *American Quarterly* 30 (1978), 224–242; Amy Gajda, "What If Samuel D. Warren Hadn't Married a Senator's Daughter? Uncovering the Press Coverage That Led to 'The Right to Privacy,'" *Michigan State Law Review* (2008), 35–60. On the rise of the penny press, see Paul Starr, *The Creation of the Media: Political Origins of Modern Communications* (New York: Basic Books, 2004).

anxious to gaze upon the remains, and speculate regarding the cause of the suicide." But many more suicides were what we would consider private affairs, as when Charles Gordon hanged himself in his barn in Concord or Charles Wolfe cut his throat at his Roxbury home in 1860. No matter – reporters covered private suicides as thoroughly as public ones. Newspapers reported on 71 of the 89 suicides of Massachusetts men in 1860.[6]

Suicide reports were scattered among stories of robberies and accidents and diseased livestock, but they carried a distinctive import. As a mystifying act, suicide called for explication. Studies of suicide accounts in the antebellum South and in Britain found them preoccupied with moralizing. British judgments were class-based – newspapers gave laborers' suicides more coverage than those among the gentry – and in both places journalists indicted victims' moral failings.[7]

No corresponding class bias appeared in Massachusetts on the eve of the Civil War – merchants and attorneys were as likely as shoemakers and day laborers to have their

---

[6] *Boston Traveler*, Aug. 16, 1860; [Worcester] *Massachusetts Spy*, June 13, 1860.

[7] David Silkenat, *Moments of Despair: Suicide, Divorce, and Debt in Civil War Era North Carolina* (Chapel Hill: University of North Carolina Press, 2011), 11–21 (these judgments applied to whites; suicide among slaves was typically seen as an act of independence); Rab Houston, "Fact, Truth, and the Limits of Sympathy: Newspaper Reporting of Suicide in the North of England, circa 1750–1830," *Studies in the Literary Imagination* 44 (2011), 93–108.

suicides reported – and judgments were gentler than in the South. A report characterized Charles Wolfe's death as "a sad case of poverty and suicide," noting that he "bid [his wife] an affectionate adieu, telling her he was sorry that his sickness had reduced her to such hardship, and that he hoped she would not have him to support much longer."[8]

Yet the larger goal of admonishment persisted. Knowing that they were expected to identify a cause, reporters in Massachusetts and their informants drew on a vocabulary of sudden moral weakness. Edmund Wiley was "deranged" when he hanged himself. Asa Adams was having a "fit of the blues" when he cut his throat. James Swett, a young man from a "highly respectable family" with "unusually correct habits," nonetheless showed "a slight aberration of mind" before he drowned himself. George Richardson likewise drowned himself "in a fit of temporary insanity." Massachusetts residents took no notice of theories of modernization; quotidian assumptions about suicide agreed with those elsewhere in locating a predisposition within the individual.[9]

Yet internal causation was only part of the explanation. News reports emphasized the sudden onset of a precipitating crisis; they implied that most people could control their impulses most of the time. An extraordinary stimulus,

---

[8] *Boston Transcript,* June 6, 1860.
[9] *Boston Courier*, Feb. 20, 1860; *Springfield Republican*, Mar. 12, 1860; *Boston Herald*, July 26, Mar. 2, 1860.

however, could provoke an "aberration" or "derangement." The crisis might be brought on by a loved one's death, as allegedly happened for Edward Day. It might come from financial troubles, as in the circumstances preceding Jefferson Robbins's hanging, or it might stem from one's own behavior, as when Peter Smith made himself "insane from the effect of a long dissipation."[10]

This was hardly an airtight schema. Journalists occasionally acknowledged longstanding health problems as suicide triggers, and they came across a few cases like that of Francis Pennell. After Pennell poisoned himself in Boston, reporters could find no apparent motive until they learned of his brother's suicide. "[Pennell] must have been affected with insanity," the report concluded, "which appears to be hereditary in his family." Yet none of these anomalies shook the widespread conviction that suicide sprang from proximate causes operating on vulnerable psyches.[11]

Suicide and the "Common Cause"

The Civil War altered the presence of suicide in Massachusetts. Commentators believed that the conflict encouraged self-destruction. "Suicides are becoming alarmingly

---

[10] *Springfield Republican*, July 30, 1860; *Lowell Citizen*, Feb. 9, 1860; *Springfield Republican*, Aug. 17, 1860.
[11] *Boston Traveler*, Dec. 26, 1860.

common," wrote one editor. "The excitement caused by the peculiar state of public affairs promotes self-murder. Men, and women too, kill themselves to get rid of their troubles now, as they did in France in Terror times."[12]

Suicide's actual incidence, however, anticipated the findings of Émile Durkheim and other researchers. Examining the drop in suicides that occurred in European wars, Durkheim brushed aside alternative explanations. The absence of soldiers during "great popular wars" could not adequately account for the fall, nor could wartime disruptions of death registration. The only cogent explanation was that since these wars "force men to close ranks and confront the common danger, the individual thinks less of himself and more of the common cause." As with modernization, this account relies extensively on conjecture. It remains influential, however, and is a point of reckoning for suicides in wartime Massachusetts.[13]

Table 3.1 shows that suicides of Massachusetts men during the Civil War never matched the number observed in 1860. A rate, rather than the number of deaths, is the

---

[12] [Boston] *American Traveler*, Oct. 25, 1862.

[13] Émile Durkheim, *Suicide: A Study in Sociology*, trans. John A. Spaulding and George Simpson (Glencoe, IL: Free Press, 1951), 208. For examples of the theory's enduring influence, see James R. Marshall, "Political Integration and the Effect of War on Suicide: United States, 1933–76," *Social Forces* 59 (1981), 771–785; David Lester and Bijou Yang, "The Influence of War on Suicide Rates," *Journal of Social Psychology* 132 (1992), 135–137.

Table 3.1. *Suicides of Massachusetts men
age 20 and older, 1860–1865*

Year	Number of suicides
1860	89
1861	60
1862	74
1863	53
1864	47
1865 (through April 30)	23

preferable measure, but no credible suicide rate can be calculated for men during the war years. The denominator should
comprise only those who were at risk to commit the act.

Wars, however, especially protracted conflicts such as
the Civil War, destabilize male populations and vitiate the
concept of a population at risk. We know, from federal and
state censuses, that Massachusetts counted 351,000 men 20
years and older in 1860, shrinking somewhat to 343,000
in 1865; it would ordinarily be a simple matter to devise
population estimates for the intervening years. But we also
know that nearly 138,000 men served in Massachusetts
army units and on the vessels of the navy in the same
years. Nor can we simply subtract these men from the civilian population. Recruits were mustered in at various times
for three years, three months, or some other term; as some
were discharged, others reenlisted, others came home on furloughs, and others deserted. A significant number of volunteers also came from other states. This churning precludes a

Table 3.2. *Suicides of Massachusetts men age 20 and older, 1856–1859*

Year	Number of suicides
1856	68
1857	70
1858	69
1859	65

plausible estimate of a Massachusetts male population at risk for suicide.[14]

As the best available measure, the number of suicides invites exploration of the war-decline thesis. Table 3.2 offers an initial perspective by showing the number of suicides for the four years preceding 1860. The wartime drop in suicides was partly an artifact of the aberration of 1860. Suicides in that year were far above the norm; the average number of deaths in the four prior years was 68. Viewed in this light, suicides in 1861 and 1862, the early years of the Civil War when residents should have been earnestly closing ranks

[14] Suicides tabulated in Table 3.1 from *Annual Reports of Vital Statistics*. The male population discussed in this paragraph and elsewhere in this study includes men age 20 years and older, even though about one-fifth of new recruits were 18 and 19 years old. These men soon reached age 20; using this age minimum maintains consistency with the study's later focus on veterans. Massachusetts's adjutant general identified the number of soldiers in Massachusetts units as 111,681 and the number of Massachusetts men who joined the navy as 26,163. Massachusetts Adjutant General, *Annual Report ... for the Year Ending December 31, 1865,* 2 vols. (Boston: Wright and Potter, 1866), I: 128, 16.

for the common good, were more typical of peacetime. Any wartime decline in suicides to be investigated was not a drop for the duration – it was a lessening only for the conflict's final two years.[15]

It is tempting to adapt the common-cause thesis to this pattern. After two years of defeat and stalemate, perhaps news of victories at Gettysburg, Vicksburg, Atlanta, and Richmond combined with the election of 1864 to deter suicide among northern men. To give the thesis a fair hearing, we will divide the war into these two phases, comparing suicides from early 1861 through mid-1863 against the victorious period that began in July 1863 and lasted through April 1865.

Even so, there is strong evidence against the thesis. In arriving at his pulling-together explanation, Durkheim dismissed the importance of absent soldiers. Suicide was so uncommon among young men, he argued, that their departure would have had only a trifling effect on any trend. The effect was hardly trifling in Massachusetts, however: men in the prime military ages of 20 to 40 accounted for more than one-third of male deaths by suicide before the war, and the departure of perhaps one-third of them inevitably reduced suicides during the conflict.[16]

---

[15] Suicides tabulated in Table 3.2 from *Annual Reports of Vital Statistics*.

[16] Durkheim, *Suicide*, 206. Suicides among men age 20–39 were 38 percent of all male suicides in the years covered in Table 3.2.

Table 3.3. *Suicides of Massachusetts women, 1856–1865*

Year	Number of suicides
1856	30
1857	22
1858	21
1859	15
1860	20
1861	23
1862	17
1863	14
1864	20
1865	21

The wartime-decline theory also rests on a concurrent trend among women. Durkheim claimed confirmation in the especially sharp drop in female suicides during European wars. Women contributed to the alleged wartime comity, and their consequent reduction in suicides demonstrates that the overall trend was not an artifact of absent soldiers. But there is no such evidence for Massachusetts. Table 3.3 shows suicides among women for the years covered by Tables 3.1 and 3.2. A sharp and steady decline did occur, but it took place in the late 1850s; during the Civil War, women's suicides rose and fell without an apparent pattern.[17]

[17] Durkheim *Suicide,* 208. Suicides tabulated in Table 3.3 from *Annual Reports of Vital Statistics.*

Behavior in cities stood as another cornerstone of the pulling-together thesis. Though social scientists cited cities as the crucibles of modern alienation, urban life allegedly fostered the wartime patriotism that discouraged suicide. City-dwellers, according to Durkheim, were "more sensitive, impressionable and also better informed on current events than the rural population," and wartime suicides predictably fell more sharply in the largest cities.[18]

Yet Boston failed to comply with this formulation. The city had contributed approximately one-fifth of Massachusetts suicides in the years preceding the Civil War. The number dropped in the metropolis during the war, but no faster than elsewhere. Boston registered 22 percent of the state's suicides in the war's first phase. In mid-1863, rather than pulling together, the city was convulsed by a bloody riot against the recently imposed federal draft. Afterward, Boston's suicides remained at 22 percent of the state's total.[19]

One conundrum remains. Older men's suicides dropped by one-fourth in the war's last two years, approximately the same decline as among younger men. Few Massachusetts men over age 40 joined the army, so absent soldiers had little effect on the older population at risk for suicide. A Durkheimian explanation would revert to the salutary

---

[18] Durkheim, *Suicide*, 208.
[19] On the 1863 riot, see William F. Hanna, "The Boston Draft Riot," *Civil War History* 36 (1990), 262–273.

effects of the war effort. Suicide was supposedly aggravated by social isolation, but the war could have fostered extraordinary bonds among civilians. Community-wide recruitment meetings engendered social ties, and middle-aged men shared the absence and loss of sons and grandsons. The later progress of the war underscored the value of these commitments and sacrifices, and should have dissuaded suicide.[20]

Some middle-aged and older men nonetheless took their own lives. The presumption of wartime solidarity implies that these were men whom an expanded sociability could not sway, who were especially resolute outsiders. Two clues to such outsiders appear in Massachusetts death records. Marriage has long been thought to deter suicide, especially among men. Durkheim termed the effect an "immunity," and the connection has influenced research down to our own time. Massachusetts clerks were required to record decedents' marital status, and their entries should show fewer married men among the later-war suicides.[21]

---

[20] Slightly fewer than 8 percent of Massachusetts enlisted men, or approximately 7,700 recruits, were age 40 or older at enlistment, as were 13 percent of officers (in all states), or approximately 700 Massachusetts men. Age figures from Benjamin A. Gould, *Ages of US Volunteer Soldiery* (New York: US Sanitary Commission, 1866), 15, 28. These soldiers were approximately 6 percent of the state's population of men age 40 and older.

[21] Durkheim, *Suicide*, 171–195. See also Enrico Morselli, *Suicide: An Essay on Comparative Moral Statistics* (New York: D. Appleton, 1882), 226–239. For a recent application, see Nick Danigelis and

Table 3.4. *Marital status and recorded parents, Massachusetts male suicides age 40 and older*

	Percentage married	Percentage with parents known
First phase of war (April 1861–June 1863)	69	83
Second phase of war (July 1863–April 1865)	75	78

Clerks were also expected to record the names of decedents' parents. These entries were primarily used for documenting children's deaths, but clerks reported parents' names for deaths of all ages. Sometimes, however, the space for parents was left blank or recorded as "unknown." These nonentries are plausible telltales of outsider status. If the undertaker or physician filing a death certificate failed to find information and the body's claimants could supply none, the deceased probably "belonged" elsewhere, to use contemporary parlance. Social scientists would classify such individuals as unintegrated, and they should be overrepresented among the suicides of the later Civil War.

Table 3.4 rebuts both expectations. Among male suicides age 40 years and older, proportionately more after mid-1863 were married; the proportion with known parents did decline, but the drop was small, leaving fewer than

---

Whitney Pope, "Durkheim's Theory of Suicide as Applied to the Family: An Empirical Test," *Social Forces* 57 (1979), 1081–1106.

one-fourth of older suicides as likely outsiders. Repeated tests of the prevailing explanation thus produce little evidence of a solidarity potent enough to dissuade suicide.[22]

"Many Elderly People Have Died"

If a supposed wartime harmony fails to account for the drop in suicide, what is preferable? One investigation of twentieth-century conflicts has argued that suicide declines originated in the economic dividend provided by wartime production. Massachusetts experienced such a boom during the Civil War. Supplying the war effort stimulated the Bay State's economy and created an unevenly distributed prosperity.[23]

Yet it is nearly impossible to determine whether general affluence affected individual decisions on suicide. Attributed suicide motives would be helpful: as we noted in the previous chapter, journalists interviewed relatives and acquaintances to discover reasons for the deaths they covered. But newspapermen joined the army too, and perhaps for that reason their papers' coverage waned. Eighty-four percent of men 40 and older had had their suicides reported in

---

[22] Marital status and parents' information for recorded suicides obtained from Massachusetts Deaths.

[23] Marshall, "Political Integration"; Thomas H. O'Connor, *Civil War Boston: Homefront and Battlefield* (Boston: Northeastern University Press, 1997), 204–209.

1860, but the wartime proportion fell to just over 50 percent. Reporters could assign a motive to fewer than two-thirds of the suicides they did cover. A drop in men with "fear of want," "pecuniary worries," and other economic troubles may have contributed to the suicide decline, but motives were too sporadically reported to indicate a trend.

A largely unnoticed late-war development may have contributed to the decline in older men's suicides. Deaths from all causes among men age 40 and older rose sharply in 1863 and 1864. Overall deaths had remained at their prewar level in 1861 and 1862, but they jumped by 26 percent in 1863, stayed at that level in 1864, and then fell back by 7 percent in 1865. The spike was fed by a rise in tuberculosis, the deadliest disease for men over age 40, but it was particularly driven by a remarkable increase in deaths from pneumonia, the second-leading killer. The number of pneumonia deaths among men over age 40 doubled in 1863, then increased by another one-third in 1864 before receding in 1865.[24]

This surge proceeded by stealth rather than by storm. State officials noted that deaths had "increased somewhat notably" in 1863, and the next year a physician in western Massachusetts reported that "he has never known so much sickness in the eastern part of [Hampshire] county as there is this year. Many elderly people have died of

---

[24] Yearly deaths from *Annual Reports of Vital Statistics*; tuberculosis was reported in nineteenth-century records as consumption or phthisis.

Table 3.5. *Overall death and suicide rates for Massachusetts men age 40 and older, 1861–1862 and 1863–1864*

	Deaths per 1,000 men, all causes	Suicides per 100,000 men
1861–1862	25	32
1863–1864	28	20

pneumonia." These were exceptions, however, to a dearth of public acknowledgment in a state preoccupied with the progress of the Civil War.[25]

It is plausible to suppose that some of the excess deaths of 1863–1864 would otherwise have been suicides, but it is imperative to avoid the kind of ex post facto hypothesizing that produced the wartime-harmony theory. Evidence should exist that deaths from other causes replaced suicides later in the war. If overall death rates and suicide rates were inverted, their relationship would suggest that other deaths sometimes averted suicides.

Since Massachusetts's male population over age 40 was little affected by army enlistments, we can return to comparing rates rather than sheer numbers of deaths. Tables 3.5 and 3.6 are based on estimates of the number of older men in each year between the federal census of 1860 and the state enumeration of 1865. Table 3.5 compares overall death

[25] *Annual Report of Vital Statistics,* 1864, 39; *Lowell Citizen,* April 21, 1864.

Table 3.6. Overall death and suicide rates for Massachusetts men age 40 and older in three regions, 1861–1862 and 1863–1864

	Deaths per 1,000, all causes, 1861–1862	Deaths per 1,000, all causes, 1863–1864	Percentage change	Suicides per 100,000, 1861–1862	Suicides per 100,000, 1863–1864	Percentage change
Boston	28	34	+21	29	14	–52
Other coastal counties	25	27	+8	24	21	–12
Inland counties	25	29	+16	47	21	–55

rates and suicide rates for older men between the war's first two and last two years. When converted to rates, the growing population attenuates the rise in overall deaths, but the trends in total deaths and suicides were nonetheless sharply inverted.[26]

The inversion should also be visible from place to place. Table 3.6 makes a geographic comparison, adapting state officials' identification of Massachusetts's regions. A rough correspondence emerges: Boston and the inland counties saw higher proportional increases in death rates and larger drops in suicides, while nonmetropolitan coastal areas experienced lesser changes in both.[27]

These comparisons share an encumbrance with all attempts to explain declines in suicide: how far can one go in investigating acts that never occurred? The credibility of the investigation surely hinges on pursuing a broad perspective; the perspectives used in this chapter point to a multilayered explanation for Massachusetts's home-front suicide decline. The decrease, occurring only in the Civil

---

[26] *Annual Reports of Vital Statistics.* When Massachusetts official statistics report deaths by age and sex, the figures are for calendar years only, so comparisons of the war's phases as discussed above are infeasible.

[27] State officials identified six regions for comparing deaths: see *Annual Report of Vital Statistics,* 1858, 194–195. The regions are combined into three in Table 3.6 to avoid too-small numbers of suicides for comparison. It will be recalled that Boston's suicide drop in 1863–1864 was described above as in line with that of the rest of the state, but that figure included men of all ages.

War's second half, bore none of the expected earmarks of a patriotic surge. The drop in younger men's suicides was surely sharpened by the absence of soldiers; diminished suicides among older men coincided with brighter prospects in a booming economy, and inversely corresponded with a spike in deaths from other causes. Suicide declines in mass-mobilization wars may be a common phenomenon, but the Bay State's experience cautions investigators to probe for uncommon contributing explanations.

"Disinclination to Return"

It would be a mistake to presume that the Civil War's effect on communities' psychological well-being was limited to its role in averting suicides. Some men who went off to the army died by suicide in the theaters of war; their numbers and circumstances are beyond the scope of this study. The ongoing conflict also disrupted the home-front psychological landscape more directly. Men were known to take their own lives in anticipation of the war. Charles Lunt had gotten no farther than a training camp near Boston when he hanged himself in 1861. Before Edward Parks could be mustered in, he drowned himself in Cambridge in 1862. Later that year Elliott Vinton, allegedly gripped by "the fear that his sons would go to the war," hanged himself in central Massachusetts.[28]

[28] *Boston Traveler*, May 20, 1861; [Worcester] *Massachusetts Spy*, Aug. 20, Oct. 8, 1862. For discussions of suicide by Civil War

Men were also known to take their own lives while on leave from the war. Returned to Massachusetts on furloughs, Wilson Pinkham and David Rogers took poison, Charles Chamberlain shot himself, and Calvin Harris died by hanging. All were older than the typical enlistment age, and all but Rogers were married (he was staying with relatives). News reports disregarded the experience of war as the cause of their suicides, but a development in Pinkham's story raised the issue. His friends wrote to insist that "domestic troubles," rather than "any disinclination to return to the seat of war," triggered his suicide. That the question had arisen indicates that some found it conceivable that war's traumas could provoke the severest possible reaction. That Pinkham's friends took offense illustrates the stigma of cowardice that readily attached to such a reaction. That Pinkham and the other suicides were older and/or married hints at the extremity of their dilemma. These men had seen what war was, and they were now safe with their families.

---

soldiers on active duty, see R. Gregory Lande, "Felo De Se: Soldier Suicides in America's Civil War," *Military Medicine* 176 (2011), 531–536; B. Christopher Frueh and Jeffrey A. Smith, "Suicide, Alcoholism, and Psychiatric Illness among Union Forces during the US Civil War," *Journal of Anxiety Disorders* 26 (2012), 769–775; Earl J. Hess, *The Union Soldier in Battle: Enduring the Ordeal of Combat* (Lawrence: University Press of Kansas, 1997), 90–91; Kathryn S. Meier, *Nature's Civil War: Common Soldiers and the Environment in 1862 Virginia* (Chapel Hill: University of North Carolina Press, 2013), 48–49.

Facing another separation and more warfare, they made a fatal choice.[29]

Extraordinary Traumas

This chapter's explorations revive previously introduced issues. The Massachusetts soldiers who killed themselves while on leave redirect our attention to the barrier we impose between suicides and nonsuicides. Married men were more likely to receive furloughs, but when they were home they encountered the choice of deserting the army or deserting their families. Many abandoned the army, and only a few chose suicide. That some did, however, underscores the extraordinary dilemma that confronted all soldiers who came home on leave.[30]

The findings here also allow us to reflect on the two opposed pillars of suicide interpretation. Discussions of rates proceed from the indisputable tendencies of suicidal behavior: marital status, place of residence, age, and other characteristics typically affect the likelihood of individuals'

---

[29] *Boston Herald*, June 21, 1862; *Barnstable Patriot*, Mar. 22, 1864; *Boston Transcript*, Nov. 19, 1862, June 3, 1864; *Boston Herald*, June 24, 1862. Pinkham was 28 at his suicide, Chamberlain was 42, and Harris and Rogers were 36. Gould, *Ages of Volunteers*, 24, reports an average of 26 for Massachusetts soldiers' age at enlistment.

[30] On furloughs and desertion, see Dora L. Costa and Matthew E. Kahn, *Heroes and Cowards: The Social Face of War* (Princeton, NJ: Princeton University Press, 2010), 100.

choosing suicide. Discussions of individual motivations proceed from the irrefutable observation that most people regardless of characteristics never commit suicide, so far more than a tendency is required to produce a self-murder. These need not be mutually exclusive perspectives – some of the best historical studies of suicide have focused on places where both rates and case studies were available.[31]

But this is more than a plea for the felicitous marriage of collective tendencies and individual motivations. In the nature of sources and interpretation, most studies, even when they explore both tendencies and motives, privilege one over the other. Our study originated in a curiosity about the duration of the Civil War's aftershocks, and proceeds by examining the behavior of veterans and the reactions of their communities. Suicide rates are indispensable for indicating changes over time, in the Gilded Age and down to our own era. Yet one need not reject their legitimacy to recognize rates' shortcomings. Rates reveal trends and invite

---

[31] A partial list of works that marry historical rates and motivations includes Victor Bailey, *"This Rash Act": Suicide across the Life Cycle in the Victorian City* (Stanford, CA: Stanford University Press, 1998); Olive Anderson, *Suicide in Victorian and Edwardian England* (New York: Oxford University Press, 1987); Howard I. Kushner, *Self-Destruction in the Promised Land: A Psychocultural Biology of American Suicide* (New Brunswick, NJ: Rutgers University Press, 1989); John C. Weaver, *Sadly Troubled History: The Meanings of Suicide in the Modern Age* (Montreal: McGill-Queen's University Press, 2009). Lane, *Violent Death,* represents a resourceful use of contrasting suicide and homicide rates to deduce motivations.

comparisons, but their potency fades in the attempt to convert them into explanations of suicide. Studies that analyze recent vital statistics illustrate the problem: variables such as marital status are associated with suicide, but everything that can be measured taken together typically accounts for a minuscule fraction of the variation in suicidal behavior.[32]

Evidence of the motives and meanings of suicide has its own limitations, which we will acknowledge as they arise in the chapters to come. Narrative sources are nonetheless indispensable guides to the tribulations that brought Civil War veterans to the point of ending their lives. We will give increasing attention to these sources in the remaining chapters, as we shift from the trials of wartime to the ordeals faced by those whose active duty was over.

[32] One example of a large-scale study is Augustine J. Kposowa, K. D. Breault, and Gopal K. Singh, "White Male Suicide in the United States: A Multivariate Individual-Level Analysis," *Social Forces* 74 (1995), 315–323. The authors used records from more than 200,000 individuals from 1979 to 1981. The value of the statistic known as Cox and Snell's R^2 for one of this study's key results is .000252, meaning that eight variables together explain .025 percent of the variation in white men's risk of suicide. The value of this statistic is influenced by the tiny fraction of men who committed suicide in the population at risk. Statistic calculated from model 1 in Table 2, p. 322. See also Joseph C. Franklin et al., "Risk Factors for Suicidal Thoughts and Behaviors: A Meta-Analysis of 50 Years of Research," *Psychological Bulletin* 143 (2017), 187–232; Olav Nielssen, Duncan Wallace, and Matthew Large, "Pokorny's Complaint: The Insoluble Problem of the Overwhelming Number of False Positives Generated by Suicide Risk Assessment," *BJPsych Bulletin* 41 (2017), 18–20.

4

Perilous Years

I t is commonly assumed that the first half-decade after any war presents veterans their severest trial. Coming home to "New England and its hum drum life" made Robert Dollard feel "like fish out of water" and impelled him to "go somewhere to again be somebody." Dollard was fortunate; the challenge for many other ex-soldiers was to function normally. Richard Lillie and William De Castro found promising employment with the Soldiers' Messenger Corps, which provided steady work for veterans with severe disabilities. Then reality intruded: De Castro slipped on a sidewalk in Boston, fell on the stump of his amputated arm, and fainted. Lillie's shoulder wound, received in one of the war's last engagements, reopened while he was working and forced him to resign from the Corps.[1]

---

[1] Robert Dollard, *Recollections of the Civil War and Going West to Grow Up with the Country* (Scotland, SD: Robert Dollard, 1906), 186;

In this chapter we will explore Union veterans' trials in the postbellum years. The period must be construed loosely – soldiers were mustered out or discharged, or deserted, throughout the Civil War and afterward – but 1870 is a reasonable closing to veterans' initial readjustment.

"They Have Preserved Their Good Names"

Chapter 1 introduced debates about the mainstream and the margins of veterans' experience and aggregate tendencies versus individual volition. Each position is a plea for perspective, reminding us to justify conclusions about a complex topic. Any meaningful survey of the postwar half-decade requires taking stock of these dialectics. The rich evidence for postbellum Massachusetts is a promising basis for the quest.

Local officials provided an especially voluble perspective on veterans' initial circumstances. City and town leaders had heard, and likely shared, presentiments of "demoralized" veterans despoiling their communities. When Massachusetts's adjutant general asked local governments in 1865 if the "habits" of veterans "have been better, or worse,

---

Boston Post, Oct. 20, 1865; *Boston Traveler*, Oct. 10, 1865. On the importance of the first five years, see, e.g., Eric T. Dean Jr., *Shook over Hell: Post-Traumatic Stress, Vietnam, and the Civil War* (Cambridge, MA: Harvard University Press, 1997), 207.

than they were before they entered the army," nearly all of the commonwealth's cities and towns expressed an opinion.[2]

Local officials achieved a consensus. In Williamstown, most veterans were "much improved as to their habits of industry and economy"; in South Scituate, selectmen were impressed by "the absence in [veterans] of that demoralization which we surely had good reason to fear"; in Pembroke, "we can but feel surprised and very much gratified that they have preserved their good names"; in Westhampton, "most of our returned soldiers have more manliness and are better men than they were before"; in Clinton, veterans "seem to be more intelligent, and morals quite as good as those who staid at home"; in Southbridge, "the *majority* have glided smoothly and splendidly into the quiet duties of civil life."[3]

A skeptic would dismiss these claims as self-interested fictions, the product of leaders boosting their communities. But reports need not be unvarnished truth to be useful. Local authorities' judgments shaped veterans' reception, and they inform our understanding of the relationship between ex-soldiers and civilians.

Assessment of veterans' readjustment hinged on a sharp demarcation. The adjutant general's survey asked about the

[2] Massachusetts Adjutant General, *Annual Report...for the Year Ending December 31, 1865*, 2 vols. (Boston: Wright and Potter, 1866), I: 141.

[3] Ibid., 209, 194, 184, 206, 153, 192 (emphasis in original).

behavior of veterans "belonging to your towns," and local officials reaffirmed the distinction. They typically limited their
approbation to "our" returned soldiers. West Cambridge was
especially emphatic, restricting its report to ex-soldiers who
were *"actual residents* of the town."[4]

Local authorities were hardly blind to veterans' potential for misbehavior. The respondent for Ipswich adminis-
tered the local prison, where nearly half of the inmates were
Civil War veterans. None came from Ipswich, however, leaving him free to declare that "we have not had any trouble
with returned soldiers in our town."[5]

These influential civilians saw a veteran population that
sorted itself into two classes. On the one hand were ex-
soldiers who returned to tight-knit communities – Leices-
ter's respondent was "personally acquainted with nearly all
the soldiers enlisted from this town" – and resumed their
lives. The other class comprised those whom one selectman
labeled "wanderers," who presumably filled prisons, occu-
pied almshouses, and gravitated to cities. Veterans wound

---

[4]   Ibid., 141, 205 (emphasis in original).
[5]   Ibid., 168. The Ipswich House of Correction had 60 male prisoners, 27 of whom were veterans. On crime and incarceration among
Civil War veterans, see Dean, *Shook over Hell*, 98–99; Betty B.
Rosenbaum, "Relationship between War and Crime in the United
States," *Journal of Criminal Law and Criminology* 30 (1940), 722–
740; Edith Abbott, "The Civil War and the Crime Wave of 1865–
1870," *Social Service Review* 1 (1927), 212–234; Eric H. Monkkonen,
Murder in New York City (Berkeley: University of California Press,
2001), 18–19, 23–25.

up in these classes through a combination of ascription and agency. Outsiders were supposedly predisposed to malefaction, and sheriffs pointed to the out-of-state and foreign origins of most of their prisoners. Yet good or bad choices could also alter outcomes: in Greenfield, "most of the foreigners return improved," while some Leominster residents who had been "steady, industrious young men" were now "dissipated" and "unwilling to work."[6]

This is one perspective on veterans' return, albeit a significant one. By cleaving ex-soldiers into friends and aliens, leading civilians helped to create an ambivalent relationship. Authorities embraced some veterans as brethren while reserving their distrust for outsiders, and they aimed to inscribe the distinction in public policy. Massachusetts's Board of State Charities warned against establishing a state soldiers' home, which would impede "the fusion of the soldier with general society." The few "respectable Americans" and "deserving foreigners" who might seek refuge would be overwhelmed by "a multitude of 'bounty-jumpers and shirks,' who want to eat but not to work." A system of federal soldiers' homes soon emerged to house veterans with disabilities, but the two-class model of veterans' nature had firmly taken root.[7]

---

[6] *Annual Report of the Adjutant-General,* I: 169, 170, 213, 216, 217, 163.

[7] Massachusetts Board of State Charities, *Second Annual Report* (Boston: Wright and Potter, 1866), xlii. Massachusetts maintained a privately funded (but state-aided) Discharged Soldiers Home in

Veterans' own perspective on their circumstances is more elusive, but they hinted at resentment of civilians' assumptions. "It was obvious that the people did not regard the veteran soldiers with the confidence that they deserved," wrote Edwin C. Bennett, a former Massachusetts officer. "The people believed that their soldiers had become addicted to the use of liquor, and would be inefficient in business." A speaker at a monument dedication denounced "petty cares and selfish ailments" that rationalized distinctions among civilian men. Courage in war was "much higher and holier than the mean virtues which make a man merely 'respectable' in common life."[8]

If outspoken ex-soldiers rejected civilian classifications, they also spurned notions of veteran solidarity. At a

---

Boston from 1862 to 1870 and opened a second home in 1882, again with shared private and public funding. See Patrick J. Kelly, *Creating a National Home: Building the Veterans' Welfare State, 1860–1900* (Cambridge, MA: Harvard University Press, 1997), 32–35; John G. B. Adams, "The Massachusetts Soldiers' Home," *New England Magazine* 6 (1890), 689–698. On the persistence of the two-class view of veterans in state and federal soldiers' homes, see James Marten, *Sing Not War: The Lives of Union and Confederate Veterans in Gilded Age America* (Chapel Hill: University of North Carolina Press, 2011), 159–198, esp. 185–186.

8   Edwin C. Bennett, *Musket and Sword, or the Camp, March, and Firing Line of the Army of the Potomac* (Boston: Coburn, 1900), 324, 326; *Springfield Republican*, Jan. 20, 1870. See also Brian M. Jordan, "'Our Work Is Not Yet Finished': Union Veterans and Their Unending Civil War, 1865–1872," *Journal of the Civil War Era* 5 (2015), 484–503.

meeting "crowded to [the Boston venue's] utmost capacity" in 1865, the "battle-scarred three years' veterans" demanded retroactive bonuses equivalent to the "lavish expenditures" bestowed on "nine months' troops and raw recruits" later in the war. "Had not the soldiers waited three years in the field, and in that time seen the nine months' men come out and return home with more bounty money than their three years' pay amounted to?"[9]

It is easy to dismiss sentiments expressed in memoirs and meetings as unrepresentative fragments. Doing so begs a question: unrepresentative of what? Ex-soldiers and civilians alike knew that there was no unified population that could be represented by a typical veteran. The preceding paragraphs illustrate the energy that was spent in the opposite direction, imposing distinctions between subgroups of veterans. Does this compulsion to demarcate confirm the recent invocations of mainstream and marginal veteran experience?

Resilience and Shared Trauma

Evidence from Massachusetts towns hints at an answer to the prior question. We have chosen two towns for close analysis, not because of any typicality but because of the certitude of their officials. If we are to give due consideration to the forgotten Civil War veterans who quietly reverted to civilian

---

[9] *Boston Herald*, Mar. 3, 1865; *Boston Transcript*, Mar. 3, 1865.

life, we should examine places where they were supposedly dominant.

The clerk of the coastal town of Marshfield was deeply satisfied with the readjustment of his veteran townsmen. In his long tenure, "not five persons have presented themselves to vote whom I did not know." Some had died and a few were still under arms, but "all the others ... have returned, and we have been astonished and pleased to see how they readily engage in peaceful and lawful pursuits." The respondent for Northborough in central Massachusetts was equally impressed. "As I know, personally, almost every man belonging to the town who went into the service," Samuel Clark could assert that ex-soldiers "have been improved by their connection with the army." Veterans' circumstances in these towns should be a benchmark for readjustment to society.[10]

The two towns were credited with nearly 400 soldiers, but officials' conception of their communities was more constrained. When multiple enlistments, recruits from other places, and deserters are removed, we are left with 146 men who were residents of the towns in the 1860 federal census and who completed their service. They approximated leaders' notion of men who "belonged," and their behavior seemingly justified the official assessments. More than three-quarters of married soldiers returned to their towns; fewer than half of single men with disability discharges, however, came back. Town fathers had reason to be pleased at this

---

[10] *Annual Report of the Adjutant-General*, I: 173–174, 181.

apparent sifting of their communities. The men with firm roots were back in place, and the perceived burden of two other groups was lightened. Single men were presumably prone to be "reckless and inclined to violate the law," and "that class of men who have lost a leg or an arm" were, in the eyes of Fall River's mayor, "worse, in a moral point of view, than they were prior to their enlistment."[11]

---

[11] Ibid., 162, 159. This view of men with an "empty sleeve" evokes civilians' ambivalence about veterans with disabilities; see Marten, *Sing Not War*, 75–77; Brian Matthew Jordan, *Marching Home: Union Veterans and Their Unending Civil War* (New York: Liveright, 2015), 105–111. Marshfield was credited with 254 enlistments and Northborough with 140. See William Schouler, *A History of Massachusetts in the Civil War*, 2 vols. (Boston: William Schouler, 1871), II: 559, 656. Analysis of the two towns began with all soldiers who claimed residence there, as listed in Massachusetts Adjutant General, *Massachusetts Soldiers, Sailors, and Marines in the Civil War*, 7 vols. (Norwood, MA: Norwood Press, 1931–1937). The recruits were sought in the 1860 federal census (US Census, 1860, Publication M653, National Archives), the 1865 Massachusetts census (Massachusetts State Census, 1865, Genealogical Society of Utah), and the 1870 federal census (US Census, 1870, Publication M593, National Archives). Soldiers were counted as residents of Marshfield or Northborough if they were listed in the 1860 census, and as returnees if they appeared in the 1865 census or the 1870 census (to allow for soldiers who had not returned by mid-1865). Death records (Massachusetts Registration of Deaths, 1841–1915, Genealogical Society of Utah, hereafter cited as Massachusetts Deaths) were also consulted to confirm that soldiers had not died before they reached home. A study of veterans in Dubuque, Iowa, found a similar rate of persistence: 52 percent of soldiers appeared in both the 1860 and 1870 federal censuses (marital status was not analyzed). Russell L.

No one should mistake these judgments for a genuine bifurcation of Union veterans. Such opinions encourage us to envision a reabsorbed majority of ex-soldiers as against a minority of misfits, but the veterans of Marshfield and Northborough actually ranged themselves along a continuum. Married men who returned to their towns were only one-fifth of the original residents, while out-migrating single men with disabilities were fewer than 5 percent of ex-soldiers. One-fifth of veterans settled elsewhere in Massachusetts or in other states, the whereabouts of 12 percent are unknown, and the remainder had other combinations of marital status, disability, and location.

Nor were these immutable categories. After his enlistment in the 7th Massachusetts Infantry expired in 1864, Caleb Bailey returned to his wife and children and his shoemaking in Marshfield. He hardly "settled down," however: Bailey soon moved with his family down the coast to Kingston, where he became a blacksmith. Frederick Twichell confounded the opposite assumption. Discharged frim the 51st Massachusetts Infantry in 1863, Twichell was missing from the 1865 census of Northborough. Twichell may have been considered a "wanderer," but he was back in Northborough to stay by 1870.[12]

Johnson, "The Civil War Generation: Military Service and Mobility in Dubuque, Iowa, 1860–1870," *Journal of Social History* 32 (1999), 791–820.

[12] For an example of the judgment that most returned veterans "have settled down into their old business," see *Annual Report of the*

Nor did these exhaust veterans' possible circumstances. Widening the scope to other towns only complicates the continuum. George Edwards came back to his family and his carpenter's trade, contributing to the official assertion that "almost to a man [Northampton's veterans] have resumed their usual occupation." Five years later, Edwards was an inmate at the Taunton Lunatic Hospital. The mayor of Charlestown may have thought of young men such as Arthur Wellington when he wrote that "I am not sure but that [local veterans] are better" than before they enlisted. After being wounded and held as a prisoner of war, Wellington returned to Charlestown, married Susan Bradley in 1865, and took a job as a bookkeeper. Yet he also justified a foreboding that darkened the mayor's appraisal: "Physically, I am sorry to say, many of the men are not as good." Wellington "complained of pain in his head," and became "depressed in mind." In May 1866, he killed himself with a pistol at the store where he worked.[13]

Adjutant General, I: 205. Information on Bailey and Twichell obtained from Adjutant General, *Massachusetts Soldiers*; Massachusetts State Census, 1865; US Census, 1870.

[13] Ibid., 180. Edwards gave his occupation as carpenter when he enlisted in 1862; he was listed as "soldier" in 1865 because he was not yet mustered out, but he was again a carpenter in his Taunton entry for 1870 and when he died of cancer five years later. Information on Edwards obtained from Adjutant General, *Massachusetts Soldiers*; Massachusetts State Census, 1865; US Census, 1870; Massachusetts Deaths. On Arthur Wellington, see *Annual Report of the*

What differentiates Bailey and Twichell from Edwards and Wellington? Recent researchers have adopted the concept of "resilience" to explore similar questions about veterans and others in our own time. Assessing people's reactions to adversity, institutionalization, and other traumas, investigators seek the characteristics, or combination of them, that foster desirable outcomes.[14]

The common-sense premise of resilience seems applicable to the past, but historical evidence is refractory. Without survey responses on veterans' life satisfaction, we are left to infer resilience from evidence on family life and material success. Yet when veterans evince such achievements, and when they offer a glimpse of their state of mind, they often deliver a sharp warning about making inferences.

Richard Lillie, the wounded veteran whom we met at the beginning of this chapter, recovered from his loss of employment. He moved to a town near Boston, married, and started his own messenger service. The venture was said to have been "quite successful": Lillie owned $1,000 in real estate by 1870. Then he lost his business, lost his sight in an accident, and saw two marriages end in separation. In 1898 Lillie committed suicide.[15]

Adjutant General, I: 152. Wellington's troubles described in *Boston Traveler*, May 5, 1866; *Boston Transcript*, May 5, 1866.

[14] For an insightful summary of resilience research's characteristics and challenges, see Michael Rutter, "Resilience as a Dynamic Concept," *Development and Psychopathology* 24 (2012), 335–344.

[15] *Boston Globe,* April 14, 1898.

Isaac Hooton likewise achieved success after four years of wartime service. He found employment in the Boston customs house, and neighbors remarked on Hooton's "happy state of mind" after he received a promotion. Shortly thereafter Hooton's wife found his body hanging in a closet.[16]

Evaluating Lillie and Hooton at one juncture would judge them resilient; evaluating them later would consign them to its opposite. Typically measured at one point in time and understood as an inner strength that one either has or lacks, resilience has little use for the ebb and flow of the life course. Yet it is difficult to understand the past without this ebb and flow. Historians' discussions of Civil War veterans typically evoke the complexities of experience, though they are also dissatisfied with a reliance on individual variation alone. They adduce patterns of behavior exhibited by "many" or "most" veterans, and they endorse the assertion that most ex-soldiers successfully readjusted. Historians convey the entirely reasonable wish to reveal the import of the portraits they assemble.[17]

We share this wish. Our approach differs primarily in the explicitness of our borrowing. From resilience research we adopt a commitment to be clear about adversities and

---

[16] *Boston Post,* May 6, 1880. Lillie's real estate holdings from 1870 US Census.

[17] Distinctive examples of historians' approach are Marten, *Sing Not War*; Paul A. Cimbala, *Veterans North and South: The Transition from Soldier to Civilian after the American Civil War* (Santa Barbara, CA: Praeger, 2015).

adaptations and to justify assertions with quantities where possible. From historical practice we adopt an attention to the varieties of human motivation and the variability of contemporary circumstances.

"Disability Sufficient to Incapacitate"

Health shaped circumstances for returned veterans. Young men had been fairly immune from the immanence of death in antebellum America. Ninety of every 100 white 20-year-olds could expect to live through the 1850s, better than the prospects of older age groups. The glaring exception to this robust health was tuberculosis, then known as consumption. The leading cause of death among all adults, consumption attacked men in their twenties with a virulence that rivaled its toll on other groups. Otherwise, young men were unlikely to need a physician or come near a hospital.[18]

---

[18] The estimated probability of dying from 1850 to 1859 was .106 for 20-year-old white men, .113 for those age 30, .143 for age 40, .217 for age 50, and .384 for 60-year-olds. Calculated from J. David Hacker, "Decennial Life Tables for the White Population of the United States, 1790–1900," *Historical Methods* 43 (2010), 71 (no corresponding estimates are available for African Americans). For an argument about the presence of death and disease (including consumption) in the mid-nineteenth century, see Mark S. Schantz, *Awaiting the Heavenly Country: The Civil War and America's Culture of Death* (Ithaca, NY: Cornell University Press, 2008), 6–37. See also Sheila M. Rothman, *Living in the Shadow of Death: Tuberculosis and the Social Experience of Illness in American History* (New York: Basic Books, 1994), 13–44; Gerald N. Grob, *The Deadly Truth:*

The Civil War imposed a new reality. Deaths and amputations have drawn the most attention from scholars, but the war also harrowed those who escaped these fates. Young men accustomed to vigorous self-reliance were struck down by wounds, injuries, and baffling sicknesses – intestinal diseases replaced consumption as the soldier's scourge – and then sent to military hospitals. Compelling drama may be rare in cases of acute diarrhea and railroad accidents, but quotidian health problems compensated with their numbers. More than half of all survivors in the EI samples had been hospitalized at least once. A third of these former patients were discharged for disability: army surgeons and commanders had determined that they had a "disability sufficient to incapacitate for military service." Young men could no longer assume any immunity from health threats. Civil War veterans had a scale and variety of disabilities that we can scarcely imagine today.[19]

A History of Disease in America (Cambridge, MA: Harvard University Press, 2009), 109–113. Based on mortality schedules from the 1860 US census, whose reliability is best for adults through middle age, the consumption death rate for males (both races) age 10–19 was 5 per 10,000, 19 for ages 20–29, 21 for ages 30–39, and 23 for men ages 40–49. Calculated from US Census Bureau, *Statistics of the United States...in 1860* (Washington, DC: Government Printing Office, 1866), xxxvi, 49. On reliability of the mortality schedules, see Gretchen A. Condran and Eileen Crimmins, "A Description and Evaluation of Mortality Data in the Federal Census: 1850–1900," *Historical Methods* 12 (1979), 1–23.

[19] Roberts Bartholow, *A Manual of Instructions for Enlisting and Discharging Soldiers* (Philadelphia: Lippincott, 1864), 213. On diarrhea

"Some New Causes of Mental Disease Have Been Introduced"

Veterans with disability discharges in the EI samples returned to their communities at the same rate as other veterans, and those who had been single before enlistment were just as likely to be married by 1870. Indicators such as these, and stories such as that of Martin Maynard, provide a reassuring perspective on the resilience of veterans with physical disabilities. Maynard was wounded in the siege of Petersburg and underwent amputation of his leg. He returned to western Massachusetts, married Emma Wright in 1871, fathered three children, and spent a productive career as a metalworker until his death in 1896.[20]

---

and similar diseases in Civil War armies, see Margaret Humphreys, *Marrow of Tragedy: The Health Crisis of the American Civil War* (Baltimore: Johns Hopkins University Press, 2013), 20–47. Information on EI sample members' discharges from EI White Troops, Urban Troops, and Colored Troops I and II (see the appendix for full citations). Fifty-four percent of all surviving sample members (i.e., those with army discharges) had been hospitalized. When reasons for these discharges were recorded in the samples, 80 percent were for disabilities other than wounds, from rheumatism to diarrhea to broken bones.

[20] Rates of return and marriage drawn from EI White Troops, Urban Troops, and Colored Troops I and II. Since most states did not conduct censuses in 1865, return in this instance is defined as living in the same county in 1870 as in 1860; white and African American veterans, with and without disabilities, returned at rates very close to the overall proportion of 61 percent. The EI samples' information on marriage was drawn from pension records (marital status was not collected in the 1860 or 1870 federal censuses); calculated rates

Table **4.1.** *Deaths from 1866 to 1870 per 1,000 veterans,
EI sample members*

	Deaths per 1,000
Whites without disability discharge	19
Whites with disability discharge	40
African Americans without disability discharge	33
African Americans with disability discharge	143

This was nonetheless a perilous time, and Maynard and others needed a measure of luck to survive. The probabilities in Table 4.1 foreshadow the later mortality that was discussed in Chapter 1. Wartime disabilities doubled the likelihood of death for white veterans and quadrupled it

---

should thus be viewed as minimums. Of those who had been single before enlistment, 23 percent of whites and 13 percent of black veterans have recorded marriages between discharge and 1870, with less than a two percentage point difference between those with and without disabilities. Information on Maynard from record of Martin Maynard, 36th Massachusetts Infantry, ID 303604063, EI White Troops. Other studies have found mixed fates for veterans with disabilities. Drawing on a sample of amputees, Jalyn O. Padilla found a frequent transition from preenlistment manual labor to clerical employment. Padilla, "Army of 'Cripples': Northern Civil War Amputees, Disability, and Manhood in Victorian America" (PhD diss., University of Delaware, 2007). Drawing on a subgroup (mostly from the Midwest) of the EI samples, Chulhee Lee found that wounds and diseases in wartime (without respect to severity), plus mortality of compatriots, were associated with less wealth held by veterans in 1870. Chulhee Lee, "Wealth Accumulation and the Health of Union Army Veterans, 1860–1870," *Journal of Economic History* 65 (2005), 352–385.

for African Americans. Most of these deaths were beyond the reach of the concept of resilience; they were the product of wartime trauma compounded by new diseases. Charles Howland died of tuberculosis in 1869, attributed to "exposure in Army." James Hall's death the next year from the same disease was blamed on "the effects of wound received in war."[21]

Martin Maynard and others in the Massachusetts sample also enjoyed the good fortune of a place to which to return. Other ex-soldiers, the "wanderers" of contemporary parlance, were less fortunate. Boston's Discharged Soldiers' Home was a focal point for these veterans. Founded in 1862 as a convalescent facility for "the suffering or homeless soldier," the home was meant to prepare veterans "for transition to an active life of self-support."[22]

A census-taker found 33 veterans at the Discharged Soldiers' Home in 1865, and 21 remained shortly before the facility's closure in 1870. They differed from Massachusetts veterans in the EI samples in unsurprising ways: more of the

[21] Hall's and Howland's causes of death from Massachusetts Deaths. Death probabilities in Table 4.1 calculated from all enlisted men in EI White Troops, Urban Troops, and Colored Troops I and II with known dates of death.

[22] [Boston] Discharged Soldiers' Home, *Third Annual Report* (Boston: George C. Rand, 1865), 15, 17. See also Kelly, *National Home*, 32–35; Leonard Bussanich, "'Will I Ever Be Fit for Civil Society Again?' The Challenges of Readjustment through the Prism of the New Jersey Soldier's Home at Newark," *New Jersey History* 127 (2013), n.p.

home's occupants were born outside Massachusetts, fewer were married, most had claimed residence in Boston or another large city at enlistment, and two-thirds had a disability discharge or a pension. They also suffered more from postwar mortality. Five of the 1865 residents were dead by the end of 1870; occupants' probability of dying, figured comparably to those given in Table 4.1, corresponds to 62 deaths per 1,000 person-years (all the residents were white).[23]

Their later lives set these men still farther apart from their fellows. Amputee John Koster was elected to the New York assembly, and Frank Rose, having lost an arm and a leg, moved to New Hampshire and found work as a barber. Yet Koster and Rose were far outnumbered by veterans such as Henry Eaton and Charles Sheerin. A back wound sent Eaton, single and in his twenties, to the Discharged Soldiers' Home and thence to the recently opened federal home in Maine (Figure 4.1). After several departures and readmissions, Eaton left for good in 1871 and found employment as a barber in Boston, where he died of tuberculosis in 1878. Sheerin, also in his twenties, suffered from an eye ailment incurred at Gettysburg. He left the Boston home and married Ellen Gilmore, but he soon took up residence in the

---

[23] Occupants identified in Massachusetts State Census, 1865. Characteristics given in this paragraph based on occupants for whom military and postwar information is available in Adjutant General, *Massachusetts Soldiers*; Massachusetts Deaths; and US censuses. Seven of the 1865 residents and three of the 1870 veterans were without such information.

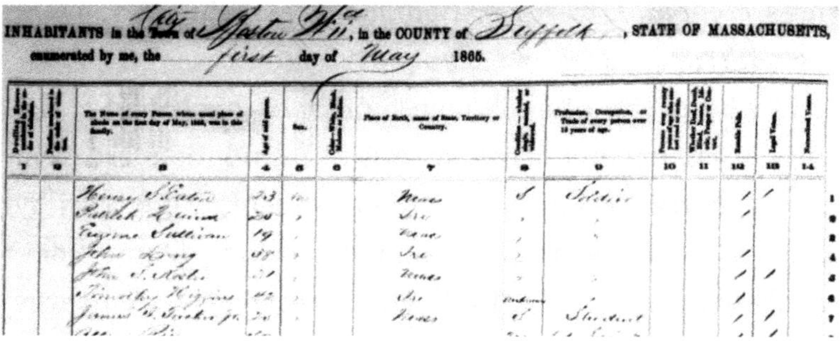

Figure 4.1. Page from the Massachusetts state census of 1865, listing some of the residents of the Discharged Soldiers Home in Boston. They include Henry Eaton and John Koster, discussed above. Microfilm Collections, Genealogical Society of Utah

Maine soldiers' home. Sheerin left the home in 1870 and returned to his family in Boston. He was listed as a laborer in the 1880 census, but his troubles worsened. Two years later he was in Boston's almshouse, where he died from heart disease and the effects of alcohol.[24]

For Eaton, Sheerin, and numerous other veterans, facilities such as the Discharged Soldiers' Home were the first stop on an institutional odyssey. Their numbers were not

[24] For a sketch of Koster's career, see Edgar L. Murlin, *The New York Red Book* (Albany, NY: James B. Lyon, 1897), 230–231. Information on Rose, Eaton, and Sheerin from Massachusetts and US censuses; Massachusetts Marriages, 1841–1915, Genealogical Society of Utah; Massachusetts Deaths; Registers of Veterans at National Homes for Disabled Volunteer Soldiers, 1866–1938, National Archives Microfilm Publication T1749, Genealogical Society of Utah.

trivial: the Boston home had sheltered more than 3,700 veterans when it closed its doors in 1870. Physical disabilities and lack of a fixed residence sometimes formed an insuperable barrier to a satisfying civilian life.[25]

The most confounding of the postwar realities was the advent of veterans' psychological illnesses. Public officials and social reformers anticipated a surge of ex-soldiers with physical disabilities, and they tailored policies and programs accordingly. Pensions, soldiers' homes, and innovative efforts such as the Soldiers' Messenger Corps signified an unprecedented level of commitment to social services, but their blueprints allowed little room for mental illness. Although any condition that hindered manual labor could earn a federal pension, disabilities enumerated in law and regulations in the initial postwar years focused on battle wounds. These strictures had their effect: in the federal soldiers' homes, where admission requirements resembled the rules for pensions, only 1 percent of residents in the late 1860s were classified as "insane." Public officials could be satisfied with their fidelity to the mission of aiding veterans with physical disabilities.[26]

---

[25] On the home's total occupants, see *Boston Advertiser*, April 5, 1870.

[26] For a description of disabilities as prioritized in law and regulations, see William Henry Glasson, *Federal Military Pensions in the United States* (New York: Oxford University Press, 1918), 131, 133. From 1867 through 1871, federal soldiers' homes housed 12,460 veterans, 169 of whom were listed as insane. Reports of the Board of Managers of the National Asylum for Disabled Volunteer Soldiers, House Misc.

The psychological mission fell to the nineteenth-century mental hospitals known as insane asylums. Though inmates in other states began showing symptoms attributable to the war, Massachusetts asylum officials appeared unperturbed. Only the superintendent of the Taunton asylum commented on ex-soldiers, and he expressed no alarm. Acknowledging in 1866 that "some new causes of mental disease have been introduced," the superintendent reported that "a few, but not many patients, have been admitted, in whom the mental disease might fairly be attributed to their connection with the great contest." He was referring to 11 new inmates who were veterans; though these men were one of every seven new admissions of relevant ages, the superintendent offered no further comments.[27]

Officials at the other Massachusetts asylums made no reference to veterans, reporting only the number of inmates

---

Doc. 54, 40th Cong., 3rd sess. (1868–69); House Misc. Doc. 86, 41st Cong., 2nd sess. (1869–70); House Misc. Doc. 226, 42nd Cong., 2nd sess. (1871–72). No report was issued in 1870–1871.

[27] Trustees of the State Lunatic Hospital at Taunton, *Thirteenth Annual Report* (Boston: Wright and Potter, 1867), 10. Ten additional veterans were identified in Taunton State Hospital Patient Register, Microfilm 2108243, Genealogical Society of Utah; since inmates with very common names were impossible to reliably link with military records, these 10 were a minimum number. On psychiatric disorders developing in other states, see Marten, *Sing Not War*, 87–89. See also Katherine K. Ziff, *Asylum on the Hill: History of a Healing Landscape* (Athens: Ohio University Press, 2012), 19, 40–41.

Figure 4.2. The State Lunatic Hospital at Taunton, Massachusetts, whose superintendent insisted that only a few Union veterans suffered from war-connected mental illness. Reproduced in *American Journal of Psychiatry* 160 (2003)

who gave their occupation as "soldier." No more than one or two inmates so identified themselves at each asylum each year, giving the impression of a mental health emergency averted. The reality was more complicated: at least 10 new admissions at Taunton in the postwar half-decade gave other occupations but had served in the Union army. This was less an emergency averted than one swept under the rug (Figure 4.2).[28]

---

[28] Officials in southern asylums similarly overlooked inmates' military service; see Diane M. Sommerville, "'Will They Ever Be Able to Forget?' Confederate Soldiers and Mental Illness in the Defeated South," in Stephen Berry, ed., *Weirding the War: Stories from the Civil War's Ragged Edges* (Athens: University of Georgia Press, 2011), 321–339.

"A Prolific Moral Cause of Insanity"?

Why would mental health officials dismiss the psychological consequences of the Civil War? Proximate and ultimate answers suggest themselves. The superintendent of the Government Hospital for the Insane in Washington, DC, explicitly addressed the war's psychological effects:

> It should not be inferred that the war has been a prolific moral cause of insanity either among the men of the land and naval forces waging hostilities against the common enemy, or among civilians of either sex or of any class. In not more than two per cent. of the four hundred and ninety-three (493) cases received from the army and navy since the war began, has even the exciting cause of mental disorder appeared to have been either the profound excitements attending a personal participation in active military hostilities prosecuted on the largest scale, a sense of great personal danger in battle, or anxiety and misgivings respecting the result of a great contest in which every man of much moral susceptibility feels the deepest personal stake.

A few inmates displayed "unsound" or "morbid mental manifestations" caused by "home-sickness" or "depression of vital forces." Yet having surveyed state asylums as well as his own institution, the superintendent concluded that the Civil War "has not been marked, as such struggles have usually been, by any increase or peculiarity of mental derangement."[29]

[29] Government Hospital for the Insane, Report of the Board of Visitors, House Ex. Doc. 1, 38th Cong., 1st sess. (1863–65), 696–697.

Asylum administrators were deeply invested in their doctrine of cause and effect. Theory and experience convinced them that intemperance and poor health were the chief culprits behind male patients' insanity. "It must still be admitted," declared one superintendent, "that intemperance is a leading special cause of insanity . . . Continued inebriety has broken down the moral power, and the brain, long kept unnaturally stimulated, at last gives way, and in a double sense the man is crazy with rum." Organic diseases were equally insidious: digestive disorders, for example, "will cloud all [a man's] worldly prospects, render him dissatisfied with life and all its blessings, make him suspicious of his friends and jealous of his own household." Conditions such as paralysis, "cerebral and spinal congestion and irritation," and "shocks to the nervous system" presumably followed a similar progression. The traumas of war were ultimately subsumed in mental health experts' taxonomy. They apparently saw no need to devise a separate classification or offer specialized treatment to veterans with psychological disorders.[30]

---

[30] Trustees of the State Lunatic Hospital at Taunton, *Eighteenth Annual Report* (Boston: Wright and Potter, 1872), 27; Trustees of the State Lunatic Hospital at Worcester, *Thirty-Fourth Annual Report* (Boston: Wright and Potter, 1867), 66, 64. See also Howard I. Kushner, *Self-Destruction in the Promised Land: A Psychocultural Biology of American Suicide* (New Brunswick, NJ: Rutgers University Press, 1989), 39–42; Dean, *Shook over Hell*, 135–142; Gerald N. Grob, *The Mad among Us: A History of the Care of America's Mentally Ill* (New York: Simon and Schuster, 1994).

A different answer is of course possible for the Civil War's failure to serve as a "catalyst of change" in psychiatric diagnosis and care. Our assumptions may be unrealistic, and war-related psychological disorders may have been rarer than we think. The most promising test of this proposition is to be found in the evidence on suicide. If comparisons between the effects of contemporary warfare and the traumas of the Civil War are overblown, confirmation should appear in accounts of Union veterans' suicides. Suicide is a rare occurrence anywhere, but rates, circumstances, and motivations offer clues about the prevalence or insignificance of war's impact on psychological distress.[31]

Fifty-nine Union army veterans died by suicide in Massachusetts from 1865 through 1870. Only one in seven of the suicides who served in Massachusetts units had been discharged for disabilities. This may mean that the range of psychological distress extended beyond the recognized list of physical infirmities, or it may imply that the Civil War had little effect on men who would have killed themselves in any case.

Table 4.2 addresses these possibilities with suicide rates from 1865 through 1870; Massachusetts veterans are compared with male civilians between ages 20 and 50. Viewed in the aggregate, Union veterans were considerably more likely to commit suicide than were their civilian peers. Though this

---

[31] For citation of World War II as an event that did inspire a new model of psychiatry, see Grob, *Mad among Us*, 191–222.

Table 4.2. *Suicide rates of Union army veterans and civilian men age 20–50 in Massachusetts, 1865–1870*

	Suicides per 100,000
Veterans	17
Civilians	12

tendency hints at stress stemming from the war, it can be no more than a collective suggestion about a supremely individual act. If something in the war drove men to suicide so soon after their return, some signs of it should appear in their particular circumstances.[32]

"Diseased in Body & Mind"

We noted in Chapter 2 the pains taken by journalists to ascribe motivations to the suicides they covered. No one should expect to find sophisticated diagnoses in these speculations by relatives and neighbors, but the same prejudices and vagaries applied to veterans as to nonveterans.

---

[32] Male suicides identified in Massachusetts Deaths, then sought in *Annual Report of the Adjutant General,* plus Historical Data Systems, Inc., US Civil War Soldier Records and Profiles, 1861–1865, http://search.ancestry.com/search/db.aspx?dbid=1138. Counts of Massachusetts civilians obtained from Massachusetts Secretary of the Commonwealth, *Abstract of the Census of Massachusetts, 1865* (Boston: Wright and Potter, 1867), 3, and US Census, 1870, with intervening years estimated by interpolation. For methods of estimating Massachusetts veterans, see the appendix.

Table 4.3. *Motives reported in the press for suicides, Massachusetts veterans and civilians age 20 to 50, 1865–1870*

Motive	Percentage civilians' reported motives	Percentage veterans' reported motives
Financial	15	10
Physical health	26	20
Mental illness	20	15
Intemperance	13	10
Failed relationship	11	40
Involved in crime	15	5
Total number of motives	*61*	*20*

Table 4.3 shows attributed motives for all veterans' and nonveterans' suicides (age 20 to 50) appearing in newspapers from 1865 through 1870. Sharp differences are evident: physical and mental health problems were nearly half of nonveterans' supposed suicide motives. Physical maladies were typically unspecified, and reporters used insanity, derangement, and similar terms to describe mental illness. For veterans, the leading motive was what we now call "relationship issues" – marital discord or rejection by a lover. John Craig returned from enlistments in the army and navy to find that "his intended was on the point of being married to another," and he poisoned himself. William and Sarah Hosmer separated in 1866, and when she "stated positively that she would not come back," he killed himself with a shotgun. Attributed motives are few and at best

suggestive, but they hint at the destructive force of wartime separations.[33]

The link between fractured relationships and veterans' suicides may be evident in our tabulation, but reporters paid little attention. They occasionally noted that a decedent had been a soldier, but apart from John Craig's case they found no explicit connections to the war. This would comport with the willed amnesia that some historians have posited for the postwar years, were it not for the press's extensive reportage of veterans' other doings. A sampling of coverage includes De Castro's and Lillie's misfortunes, public meetings to advocate veterans' political action, a dispute between veteran buskers and business owners, a gang-rape by ex-soldiers, and the full text of an address on "The Glory of the Private Soldier."[34]

Veterans were hardly invisible, but the public imagination performed a subsumption not unlike that of asylum officials. Newspaper readers expected to see suicide motives that were relevant to their own experience.

[33] *Boston Herald*, June 16, 1865; *Springfield Republican*, Sept. 8, 1866.

[34] *Boston Herald*, Mar. 3, 1865, Sept. 19, 1866, Nov. 26, 1867; *Boston Journal*, Sept. 18, 1866; *Boston American Traveler*, Aug. 19, 1865; *Springfield Republican*, Jan. 20, 1870. On postwar amnesia, see Gerald F. Linderman, *Embattled Courage: The Experience of Combat in the American Civil War* (New York: Free Press, 1987), 266–275; Marten, *Sing Not War*, 245–285. For a dissenting view, see Jordan, *Marching Home*, 68–71.

Proximate triggers such as marital strife and temporary depression touched a chord, and veterans' suicide motivations were either channeled into a conventional category or given up as unknown. After Hiram Tillson shot himself in 1865, a reporter concluded that "no reason is assigned for the act." When William Callan hanged himself a year later, "no cause except mental despondency" could be found.[35]

Yet there were other observers whose interest in ultimate causes matched the public's fixation on proximate ones. Widows sought pensions on the grounds that line-of-duty disabilities had caused their husbands' suicides. Pension officials agreed in principle: "Suicide in a fit of insanity, superinduced by disease contracted in the line of his duty, entitles the widow to a pension." In practice, administrators were skeptical of applicants' self-interest. Margaret Callan's application was rejected for lack of a physician's endorsement, whereupon she responded with an account that supplied particulars absent from the newspaper report of her husband's suicide:

> Although [William] was at times suffering from mental depression occasioned by severe pains in his head and wounded arm, and from his disabled condition and

[35] *Boston Transcript*, Apr. 21, 1865; *Boston Herald*, July 9, 1866. On newspaper coverage of suicides (especially in the antebellum period), see Kathleen M. Brian, "'The Weight of Perhaps Ten or a Dozen Human Lives': Suicide, Accountability, and the Life-Saving Technologies of the Asylum," *Bulletin of the History of Medicine* 90 (2016), 583–610.

consequent poverty, he did not seek medical advice; having no means to pay a physician, and the wants of his family prevented his treatment in hospital, being obliged to follow his avocation as a public messenger for the maintenance of himself and family.

The Pension Office remained unmoved, and Callan dropped her claim. Amelia Tillson had the requisite physician's testimony, which made a similar case about Hiram's death: "[Tillson's hip wound] caused insanity which caused him under the depression of mind caused by the same to take his life." Eight other Massachusetts widows likewise convinced the Pension Office that their husbands' pre-1871 suicides were traceable to the war."[36]

The prevalence of wounds and disease and the inability of physicians to manage their effects thus contributed to veterans' suicide rate. Can we similarly assess traumas that were mainly psychological? In our time we identify "moral injury" as a cause and posttraumatic stress disorder as a symptom of veterans' mental distress; Civil War terminology included "soldiers' heart" and "irritable spine." Caution

---

[36] Henry C. Harmon, *A Manual of the Pension Laws* (Washington, DC: W. H. O. Morrison, 1867), 184; Affidavit of Margaret Callan, Sept. 24, 1868, Pension File of William Callan, 16th Mass. Infantry, RG 15, National Archives; Affidavit of M. E. Simmons, Dec. 30, 1867, Pension File of Hiram O. Tillson, 32nd Mass. Infantry, RG 15, National Archives. These nine pensioners were one-third of the widows left by Massachusetts veterans who died by suicide from 1865 to 1870.

is in order: we should not impose a false distinction between physical and psychological traumas when we know that they were likely to coincide. Nor should we expect extensive evidence on psychological illness. Lacking a popular vocabulary for war-induced psychosis, finding no inclination by asylum officials to modify established wisdom, and facing distrustful pension officials, veterans had little incentive in the early postwar years to share distinctive mental traumas.[37]

A rare glimpse of psychological distress, however, emerges from the experience of Harrison Horr. He and his older brother Charles enlisted in the 31st Massachusetts Infantry in 1861 and served in the Western theater until 1864. A comrade recalled that the Horr brothers were among a detachment pursuing Confederate guerrillas along the

---

[37] Chapter 6 describes the pension system's increased acknowledgment of mental illness in later years. A disincentive that did not change was the legal restriction of Union army pensions to veterans with honorable discharges. It has been suggested in our own time that veterans with other-than-honorable discharges are more vulnerable to mental illness and suicide. See "A Lifeline for Troubled Veterans," *New York Times,* Mar. 11, 2017; Mark A. Reger et al., "Risk of Suicide among US Military Service Members Following Operation Enduring Freedom or Operation Iraqi Freedom Deployment and Separation from the US Military," *JAMA Psychiatry* 72 (2015), 561–569. Dishonorable discharges were the Union army's version of other-than-honorable separation; only one of the 50 dishonorably discharged Massachusetts veterans (as listed in *Massachusetts Soldiers, Sailors, and Marines*) who died in the Bay State committed suicide (in 1883). On Civil War–era terminology for psychological disorders, see Dean, *Shook over Hell*, 115–134.

lower Mississippi River. Divided into two wings, the men approached the Confederates' camp. According to a comrade, "In the darkness the flanking party was mistaken for Confederates shots were exchanged and Charles H. Horr was killed, as was supposed by his Brother Harrison Z. Horr...I know that Harrison Z. Horr grew melancholy as he considered his Brothers fate. That he blamed himself for it. That he spurned every effort of comrades to console him." Horr "left the service with a broken constitution diseased in body & mind." He survived the initial postwar years, but his friend had already noticed Horr's "tendency to insanity and an early death." He shot himself in 1876.[38]

This is the best exegesis of war's shocks and postwar consequences in our investigations of Civil War veterans. We have no basis for speculation about similar experiences among other soldiers, except to observe that half of the Massachusetts veterans who died by suicide through 1870 had no record of wounds or significant disease. We suspect that lurking behind carefully contrived veterans' narratives are additional instances of wartime trauma and postwar anguish.

---

[38] Affidavits of Marshall Clothier, Nov. 26, 1894, May 23, 1892, Pension File of Harrison Z. Horr, 31st Massachusetts Infantry, RG 15, National Archives. Horr also suffered from the effects of malaria. For an astute description of moral injury and its relation to PTSD, see Rita N. Brock and Gabriella Lettini, *Soul Repair: Recovering from Moral Injury after War* (Boston: Beacon, 2012), xiii–xviii.

As a Miner's Canary

The first years after the Civil War imposed multiple perils on a vulnerable population. Good luck beforehand was a key component in postwar reacclimation. If soldiers had had a stable enough residence to be counted in the 1860 census, and if they escaped serious wounds and debilitating diseases, they were quite likely to come home with good prospects.

Insofar as our image of readjusted veterans depicts stalwart men who "gave an especial flavor to the life of the village," it is an image of the residents of Marshfield and Northborough described in this chapter. The image has little room for the "wanderers" who typically enlisted in major cities. It has less room for returnees with major disabilities who drifted from institution to institution and died in obscurity. And the image of the readapted veteran is the antithesis of the ex-soldier whose physical and mental pains drove him to suicide.[39]

Is there a "reality" that is preferable to this image? If this chapter has a central point, it is a clear negative to this question. Veterans' lives followed very different trajectories, paths that could change, as William De Castro and Richard Lillie discovered, from one day to the next. Few veterans took the path to suicide, but we have tried to indicate that it functioned as a miner's canary – an incidence above that for

[39] Bruce Catton, quoted in Linderman, *Embattled Courage*, 280.

nonveterans, signaling psychological distress extending well beyond actual suicides. The ex-soldiers who survived the initial years were relatively young men, expected to support a family. To what extent did the Civil War's legacy alter their lives into middle age? This is the topic of the next chapter.

5

Aftershocks

The experiences of war are singularly intense, creating bonds among veterans and barriers against civilians. We gain inklings of these experiences when some veterans bridge the barriers by publicizing their recollections in memoirs, interviews, and fiction. Historians have mined the nineteenth century's version of these recollections, revealing a continuum from flag-waving to realism to embittered alienation.[1]

---

[1] Explorations of veterans' reminiscences include James Marten, *Sing Not War: The Lives of Union and Confederate Veterans in Gilded Age America* (Chapel Hill: University of North Carolina Press, 2011), 245–285; Gerald F. Linderman, *Embattled Courage: The Experience of Combat in the American Civil War* (New York: Free Press, 1987), 275–284; Earl J. Hess, *The Union Soldier in Battle: Enduring the Ordeal of Combat* (Lawrence: University Press of

Our purpose in this chapter is different. Acknowledging the value of veterans' public reminiscences, our interest turns to those whose war experiences remained internal. It is daunting to seek war's repercussions among men who declined to discuss them, but resources exist. Veterans' encounters with social services produced glimpses of the Civil War's aftershocks, and when ex-soldiers committed suicide their tribulations entered the public domain. This chapter explores these aftershocks among veterans who entered middle age in the last third of the nineteenth century.

"Shocked by the Cold-Blooded Proposal"

In the nature of reminiscences, Civil War veterans were far more likely to publicize fond memories than to share traumas and disillusionment. Positive recollections probably dominated veterans' inner feelings as well: the Grand Army of the Republic, devoted to fraternal commemoration

---

Kansas, 1997), 158–190; Carol Reardon, "Writing Battle History: The Challenge of Memory," *Civil War History* 53 (2007), 252–263; David W. Blight, *Race and Reunion: The Civil War in American Memory* (Cambridge, MA: Harvard University Press, 2001), 211–254; Brian M. Jordan, *Marching Home: Union Veterans and Their Unending Civil War* (New York: Liveright, 2015), 83–95; Craig A. Warren, *The Scars to Prove It: The Civil War Soldier and American Fiction* (Kent, OH: Kent State University Press, 2009); John Pettegrew, "'The Soldier's Faith': Turn-of-the-Century Memory of the Civil War and the Emergence of Modern American Nationalism," *Journal of Contemporary History* 31 (1996), 49–73.

and mutual support, represented more than 40 percent of Union veterans at its peak, and tens of thousands of ex-soldiers shared war stories at reunions.[2]

But preponderance is not the whole. Ambrose Bierce and others described battlefield horrors to remind readers that war was not all adventure. They also strike a chord with those interested in more recent conflicts. Consider this description by Bierce:

> [A mortally wounded sergeant] lay face upward, taking in his breath in convulsive, rattling snorts, and blowing it out in sputters of froth which crawled creamily down his cheeks, piling itself alongside his neck and ears. A bullet had clipped a groove in his skull, above the temple; from this the brain protruded in bosses, dropping off in flakes and strings. I had not previously known one could get on, even in this unsatisfactory fashion, with so little brain. One of my men, whom I knew for a womanish fellow, asked if he should put his bayonet through him. Inexpressibly shocked

---

[2] Hess, *Union Soldier*, 158–190; Blight, *Race and Reunion*, 243–251; Marten, *Sing Not War*, 126–133, 281–284. The GAR had nearly 428,000 members in 1890, when the federal census counted 1,034,000 Union veterans. *Journal of the Twenty-Fourth Annual Session of the National Encampment, Grand Army of the Republic* (Detroit, MI: Richmond and Backus, 1890), 7; US Census Office, *Report on Population of the United States at the Eleventh Census* (Washington, DC: Government Printing Office, 1897), Pt. II, 803. See also Stuart McConnell, *Glorious Contentment: The Grand Army of the Republic, 1865–1900* (Chapel Hill: University of North Carolina Press, 1992).

by the cold-blooded proposal, I told him I thought not; it was unusual, and too many were looking.

The incident is from the Battle of Shiloh, but it could have come from any number of wars. Such accounts encourage those who would seek associations between past and current veterans' plight. If Civil War veterans could sound modern, might the posttraumatic burden carried by their more reticent comrades be similarly modern?[3]

"A Full Symptom-Picture of Each Case"

To gather information for adjudicating pensions, the federal government devised schedules for identifying Union veterans and their widows in the 1890 census. These schedules fared better than did the regular census returns – nearly all of the latter were lost in a fire, but veterans' schedules are extant for more than half the states.[4]

---

[3] Russell Duncan and David J. Klooster, eds., *Phantoms of a Blood-Stained Period: The Complete Civil War Writings of Ambrose Bierce* (Amherst: University of Massachusetts Press, 2002), 103–104; Drew G. Faust, *This Republic of Suffering: Death and the American Civil War* (New York: Knopf, 2008), 196–200.

[4] Most of the veterans' special schedules for Alabama through Kentucky have been lost, but those for the remaining states are intact; the disappearance was apparently unrelated to the 1921 fire that destroyed the 1890 regular census schedules. See Kellee Blake, "'First in the Path of the Firemen': The Fate of the 1890 Population Census," *Prologue* 28 (1996), 164–181.

This census registered a continuation of circumstances from the immediate postwar years. Those fortunate enough to belong to a community before the war and to emerge without a disability were positioned for a life as community pillars. Among Massachusetts men with known 1860 residences in the EI samples, three-quarters of those without a dischargeable disability were alive in 1890, and nearly two-thirds of the survivors lived in Massachusetts. Soldiers discharged for disability were equally likely to remain in Massachusetts, but fewer than two-thirds survived to 1890.[5]

The 1890 census found other surviving veterans who were less fortunate. While the population schedules were still intact, census officials compiled statistics on "defective" individuals. Enumerators identified 106,000 Americans as "insane," including approximately 2,900 Union

---

[5] Massachusetts veterans in the EI samples (see the appendix for full citations of the samples) were sought in US Census of Union Veterans and Widows of the Civil War, 1890, National Archives Microfilm Publication M123, Genealogical Society of Utah, and in Massachusetts Registration of Deaths, 1841–1915, Genealogical Society of Utah. Sixty-four percent of surviving veterans without disability discharges were still in Massachusetts; 25 percent had moved to other states, 4 percent were in soldiers' homes, and the whereabouts of the remainder are unknown. Thirty-six percent of sample members with disability discharges had died; 73 percent of the survivors were still in Massachusetts, 15 percent had moved to other states, 7 percent were in soldiers' homes, and the whereabouts of the remainder are unknown.

Table 5.1. *Rates of "insanity" in the 1890 federal census, Union veterans and civilian men age 40–79*

	"Insane" individuals per 10,000
Nonveterans	46.7
Veterans	28.6

veterans. These were a tiny fraction of more than 1 million surviving veterans, but they present a conundrum. Table 5.1 shows insanity rates for veterans and civilian men of comparable ages. Veterans had a considerably lower incidence of reported insanity than did nonveteran peers. These rates seem to belie claims of war-induced mental illness, but the lesson of census statistics points in a different direction.[6]

Census information on insanity was a combination of self-reporting and institutional disclosure. Informants answered the query about "whether [each person was] defective in mind" for individuals in their household, and asylum administrators presumably opened their inmate registers

---

[6] Statistics on insane individuals in 1890 from US Census Office, *Report on the Insane, Feeble-Minded, Deaf and Dumb, and Blind in the United States at the Eleventh Census* (Washington, DC: Government Printing Office, 1895), 157, 236. We are aware that despite some overlap, nineteenth-century "insanity" and twenty-first-century "mental illness" are not synonyms. Throughout this study, we use *insanity* to refer to historical designations and *mental illness* to imply a modern perspective.

for enumerators. Without the population schedules we can do little more to investigate the 1890 census, but the previous census offers a comparable opportunity.

The 1880 enumeration included a box to be checked for insane individuals. There was no provision for identifying Civil War veterans, but the EI samples include information for veterans who were traced to the census. Twenty-eight sample members were identified as insane in the 1880 census, a rate of 20 per 10,000 veterans compared to 44 per 10,000 US men age 40 and older.[7]

But pension physicians had diagnosed an additional 36 sample members as insane before 1880, who should have been so identified in the census. Including these veterans would raise the insanity rate to equal the incidence for all men, but it would nonetheless create an incomplete picture of veterans' conditions. Pension examinations could identify mental illness only in the minority of veterans who applied before 1880, leaving an unknown number with psychological disorders. This "dark figure" can be estimated with capture–recapture, the technique discussed in Chapter 2 that considers which sources recorded which cases. This technique produces an estimate of 90 additional

[7] Male population in 1880 from US Census Office, *Statistics of the Population of the United States at the Tenth Census* (Washington, DC: Government Printing Office, 1883), 548–549; number classified as insane from US Census Office, *Report on the Defective, Dependent, and Delinquent Classes ... at the Tenth Census* (Washington, DC: Government Printing Office, 1888), 45.

EI sample members who could have been recorded as insane. Adding them to the veterans who were actually identified would result in an insanity rate more than double that of civilians.[8]

There were undoubtedly civilians with mental illnesses who went unacknowledged by census-takers as well. There is no comparable means of estimating their number, except for the observation that the 1880 census was the best federal count of the insane before the practice was discontinued at the turn of the century. Using special schedules and surveying physicians in 1880, the Census Bureau found more than twice as many insane individuals as in 1870. Officials in Illinois, the harshest critics of the 1870 count, accepted the 1880 results as reasonable. Yet our estimate suggests that more than half of mentally ill veterans went unidentified in any source. Though this evidence is at best suggestive, it hints at veterans' exceptional reluctance, abetted by household members answering on their behalf, to reveal psychological distress. Even more than other men their age, Union

---

[8] Capture–recapture is described in Chapter 2. In the present case, the number of insane veterans in the EI samples who were identified in the 1880 census only (20) was multiplied by the number identified through 1880 in pension examinations only (36), with the result divided by the number appearing in both places (8), to produce an estimate of 90 unidentified insane veterans. Approximately 14,400 members of the EI samples were found in the 1880 census; the 154 actual and estimated cases of insanity produces a rate of 107 cases per 10,000 veterans, compared to 44 per 10,000 US adult males.

veterans and their families seem to have been unwilling to risk the stigma of mental illness.[9]

If veterans managed to withhold information from census-takers, they could not be so reticent with physicians. The examinations referred to above were typically conducted by three-member panels of physicians appointed by the Pension Bureau and charged with producing "a full symptom-picture of each case." The examinations often produced observations on applicants' mental condition, hinting at the occurrence of mental illness as it was understood at the time.[10]

---

[9] On procedures in 1880, see Frederick H. Wines, *Report on the Defective, Dependent, and Delinquent Classes* (Washington, DC: Government Printing Office, 1888), ix–x. An analysis of the 1870 census maintained that 31 percent of insane persons were missed in Illinois. Calculated from Board of State Commissioners of Public Charities of the State of Illinois, *Third Biennial Report* (Springfield, IL: State Journal, 1875). On Illinois's approval of the 1880 result, see Board of State Commissioners of Public Charities of the State of Illinois, *Seventh Biennial Report* (Springfield, IL: H. W. Rokker, 1883), 102–105. On discontinuation of a comprehensive count of the "insane" after 1890 (after 1880 for our purposes, since the 1890 population schedules are lost), see US Census Office, *Insane and Feeble-Minded in Institutions, 1910* (Washington, DC: Government Printing Office, 1914), 11–14.

[10] US Pension Office, *Instructions to Examining Surgeons for Pensions* (Washington, DC: Government Printing Office, 1884), 9. Medical examinations through the 1870s were carried out by single physicians in smaller communities, but by the 1880s three-member boards were mandatory; see Claire Prechtel-Kluskens, "'A Reasonable Degree of Prompitude': Civil War Pension Application

The EI samples summarize the records of more than 24,000 white Union veterans who applied for pensions (the experience of African Americans is the subject of Chapter 6). Our immediate focus is on the 14,200 men examined before 1890, while pensions were limited to disabilities attributable to wartime service.[11]

The typical examination began with the applicant's description of his disability, continued with the physical assessment, and concluded with the physicians' findings as recorded on an "examining surgeon's certificate." These encounters were orchestrated arbitrations of cause and effect. Applicants were usually coached by "claim agents," entrepreneurs who assisted pension-seekers in return for a fee.[12]

Claimants' statements gave the date and place of their wound or onset of disease, and explained how the resulting disability hindered manual labor. For their part, physicians worked under progressively explicit instructions from the Pension Bureau. By the mid-1880s the directives had

---

Processing, 1861–1885," *Prologue* 42 (2010), 26–35. See also Peter Blanck, "Civil War Pensions and Disability," *Ohio State Law Review* 62 (2001), 109–238.

[11] These veterans were included in the EI White Troops and Urban samples.

[12] More than three-quarters of pension applicants used the services of claim agents; see Larry M. Logue and Peter Blanck, *Race, Ethnicity, and Disability: Veterans and Benefits in Post–Civil War America* (New York: Cambridge University Press, 2010), 123.

become sufficiently detailed to include "diseases of the nervous system." Officials allowed that identifying conditions such as insanity "is confessedly difficult," but they expected physicians to "employ all the modern methods of diagnosis." Hewing to the priorities of pension laws, applicants and physicians emphasized wounds and physical diseases, but mental illness became increasingly important.[13]

Physicians found symptoms of mental illness (insanity, mania, depression, and the like) in 4.5 percent of EI white sample members they examined through 1890. This apparently trifling proportion enlarges in comparison with census findings: 4.5 percent is 450 per 10,000, which far exceeds the rates of insanity shown in Table 5.1. Jay Baldwin, who in 1881 was found to be suffering from "periods of insanity" accompanied by violent tendencies, had no notation to that effect in the 1880 census or the 1890 veterans' schedule. Henry Mulford was diagnosed with insanity several times in the 1880s, yet his condition went unreported in the 1880 federal and 1885 Iowa state censuses. Physicians concluded that William Moering's "passions, conscience, and will [were] about obliterated," but the 1880 and 1890 censuses were silent on his condition. A similar mass assessment would undoubtedly have yielded unreported mental illness among civilians, but they were free from the effects of projectile

---

[13] US Pension Bureau, *Instructions to Examining Surgeons for Pensions* (Washington, DC: Government Printing Office, 1887), 12.

wounds and prison camp mistreatment that plagued many veterans.[14]

[14] Data collectors for the EI samples transcribed claimants' statements and relevant parts of physicians' findings verbatim and noted physicians' references to various conditions including mental illness. The full list of conditions in the present analysis includes anxiety, delusions, dementia, depression, hallucinations, hysteria, mania, paranoia, psychosis, suicidal or homicidal references, violent tendencies, and insomnia; we excluded epilepsy and the results of sunstroke (see Chapter 6). Baldwin (14th Vermont Infantry, ID 601407012), Mulford (54th Ohio Infantry, ID 2405404071), and Moering (63rd Ohio Infantry, ID 2406305094) were members of the EI White Troops sample whose details were included in the certificates. A multivariate analysis of variables associated with a mental illness finding would in principle be useful in explaining the results, especially since sample compilers provided statistics on company mortality during the war. These statistics have been used elsewhere as a proxy for wartime stress; see Judith Pizarro, Roxane C. Silver, and JoAnn Prause, "Physical and Mental Health Costs of Traumatic War Experiences among Civil War Veterans," *Archives of General Psychiatry* 63 (2006), 193–200; Chulhee Lee, "Wealth Accumulation and the Health of Union Army Veterans, 1860–1870," *Journal of Economic History* 65 (2005), 352–385; Dora L. Costa and Matthew E. Kahn, "Health, Wartime Stress, and Unit Cohesion: Evidence from Union Army Veterans," *Demography* 47 (2010), 45–66. Diagnosis of nervous disorders presents an intractable problem, however: veterans of high-mortality units, who were more likely to have been wounded themselves, also tended to seek pensions soon after the war, before physicians were advised to assess applicants' mental condition. Nearly half of pre-1890 mental disorders were diagnosed in the latter 1880s, after many veterans from high-mortality units had already been awarded pensions.

Chronic Postbellum Neurokinesis

Did no one notice? A likely cornerstone of the belief in the current prevalence of posttraumatic stress disorder is nineteenth-century experts' apparent silence about Civil War veterans. Medical men found anxiety disorders among active-duty Civil War soldiers, among lawyers and physicians, and among victims of European industrial accidents. Determined to fit these illnesses into the organic-origin paradigm, discoverers devised labels such as "irritable heart," "neurasthenia," "railway spine," and "traumatic neurosis." Historians have probed the work of these researchers, but findings by two veterans' advocates have gone all but unnoticed (Figure 5.1).[15]

[15] See, e.g., Eric T. Dean Jr., *Shook over Hell: Post-Traumatic Stress, Vietnam, and the Civil War* (Cambridge, MA: Harvard University Press, 1997), 130–131; Barbara Sicherman, "The Uses of a Diagnosis: Doctors, Patients, and Neurasthenia," *Journal of the History of Medicine and Allied Sciences* 32 (1977), 33–54; Ralph Harrington, "On the Tracks of Trauma: Railway Spine Reconsidered," *Social History of Medicine* 16 (2003), 209–223; Paul Lerner, "From Traumatic Neurosis to Male Hysteria: The Decline and Fall of Hermann Oppenheim, 1889–1919," in Mark S. Micale and Paul Lerner, eds., *Traumatic Pasts: History, Psychiatry, and Trauma in the Modern Age, 1870–1930* (New York: Cambridge University Press, 2001), 140–171. Jacob Da Costa termed the stress-related condition that he observed among Civil War soldiers "irritable heart." Da Costa occasionally followed sufferers afterward, but he postulated primarily physical causes and symptoms. J. M. Da Costa, "On Irritable Heart: A Clinical Study of a Form of Functional Cardiac Disorder and Its Consequences," *American Journal of Medical Sciences* 61 (1871), 17–52.

(a)

(b)

Figure 5.1. Two physicians who treated soldiers and veterans.
(a) Jacob M. Da Costa coined the "irritable heart" diagnosis;
(b) S. Weir Mitchell (in foreground), best known for diagnosing "hysteria" among nineteenth-century women, here demonstrates his technique for examining a wounded veteran. (a) from Countway Center for the History of Medicine, Harvard University; (b) from Anna Robeson Burr, *Weir Mitchell: His Life and Letters*

Isaac Stearns, who had been an assistant surgeon with the 22nd Massachusetts Infantry and examined pension applicants afterward, described their distinctive maladies in 1888. Stearns had met "many soldiers of the late war who have various trains of symptoms which cannot be grouped in any way so as to give any known name to the disease." He found that "even after this interval of time," some veterans displayed "a susceptibility to unfavorable impressions," accompanied by "sleeplessness, irresolution, involving a spirit of unrest, and with a loss of power to concentrate the thoughts or energies." This syndrome, the result of poor diet, extreme physical exertion, disease, and "severe mental strain," was inadequately captured by the conventional diagnosis of neurasthenia. Adapting a British surgeon's concept for a disordered nervous system, Stearns proposed to name the condition "chronic post bellum Neurokinesis."[16]

Horace Porter, chief medical officer for the Grand Army of the Republic in Kansas (and soon to hold the same post for the national organization), endorsed Stearns's findings the next year. "The life of our soldiers of the late war was one continuous hardship to the nervous system," Porter declared. "The Neurokinesis of battle" was compounded by "hundreds of hours of the brain tension of expected danger" and by "the tiresome watches of sleepless nights," and worsened by disease, the torments of Confederate prisons, and the lingering

[16] I. H. Stearns, "A New Name for an Old Veteran's Disease," *Medical Summary* 10 (1888), 49–50.

distress of battle wounds. The "nervous defects" that veterans suffered were, in Porter's view, symptoms of an "incurably diseased nervous system." He agreed with Stearns that "long intervals of time may exist betwixt the infliction of the injury and the after effects" (Figure 5.2).[17]

Stearns's and Porter's findings achieved little influence, and they were forgotten by the time shell shock became a subject for investigation in World War I. Their remarks were presented as observations rather than as treatises, and their fixation on organic causes broke no new ground. They also neglected to exploit the original contribution implicit in their remarks. The delayed onset of mental illness was potentially damaging to the physical-cause theory. In the theory's logic and in most case studies, immediacy of symptoms confirmed damage to the nervous system. Stearns and Porter presented no systematic case studies of their own, nor did they suggest that "susceptibility to unfavorable impressions" might have caused rather than reflected mental illness. They nonetheless deserve recognition for their

---

[17] Horace P. Porter, "The Common Nervous Trouble of Old Soldiers," *Leonard's Illustrated Medical Journal* 10 (1889), 22. Porter believed that Stearns's diagnosis was more applicable to the cause than the effect of the disorder, which Porter termed "neural atrophy." To our knowledge, the only historian who has attended to either Stearns or Porter is Barbara Gannon, who discusses Porter's speech in *The Won Cause: Black and White Comradeship in the Grand Army of the Republic* (Chapel Hill: University of North Carolina Press, 2011), 137.

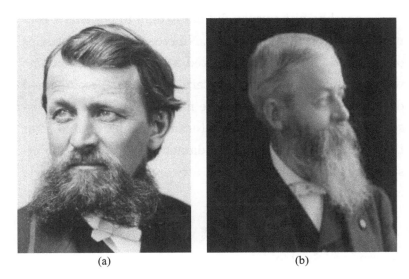

(a)   (b)

Figure 5.2. Two physicians who attempted to publicize Civil War veterans' anxiety disorders. (a) Isaac H. Stearns, formerly a surgeon with the 22nd Massachusetts Infantry, proposed "chronic post bellum neurokinesis" as a diagnosis; (b) Horace P. Porter, a wartime surgeon and later surgeon general of the Grand Army of the Republic, warned that veterans' nervous disorders "have been almost entirely overlooked." (a) from State Library of Massachusetts, Legislators' Photographs Collection; (b) from Ralph M. Munroe Family Papers, University of Miami Library

attempt to publicize the psychological illnesses of Civil War veterans.[18]

---

[18] For case studies of trauma typically followed closely by various neuroses, see S. V. Clevenger, *Spinal Concussion* (Philadelphia: F. A. Davis, 1889), 119–158. Clevenger recognized that some cases might

The publicity, however, did not extend to positing a connection with veterans' suicides. Nineteenth-century studies of traumatic neuroses recognized a link to suicide, but no warnings about suicide as a veterans' problem accompanied descriptions of their distinctive mental illnesses. Two possibilities exist: either Union veterans' suicides abated after the crucial early years, or fundamentally different understandings of suicide precluded a twenty-first-century-style concern for ex-soldiers' fate.[19]

Veterans and Suicide

Veterans' risk of suicide did not abate. Table 5.2 shows suicide rates for Massachusetts veterans and civilian men at census years in the nineteenth century's last three decades. The rates point to key dynamics of suicide. Its reported incidence rose as men grew older and as death registration improved (the latter trend is discussed in Chapter 2). Trends were also interrupted: suicides among civilians and veterans alike increased during the economic panic of the 1870s

---

involve delayed onset of neuroses due to "degenerations that had slowly, but surely, been induced"; such delays might be "several weeks or months," or an unspecified "very long time" (317). It is unlikely, however, that he envisioned the quarter-century that had elapsed since the Civil War.

[19] On neuroses and suicide, see, e.g., ibid., 172–174.

Table 5.2. *Suicide rates for Massachusetts veterans and civilian men in state and federal census years, 1870–1900*

	Veterans' suicides per 100,000	Civilian men's suicides per 100,000
1870	22	12
1875	46	21
1880	30	19
1885	43	25
1890	36	24
1895	91	34
1900	71	43

and receded thereafter, only to peak again during the harder times of the 1890s.[20]

Table 5.2's striking feature is the consistent difference between veterans and civilians. Massachusetts ex-soldiers took their own lives in much higher proportions than did nonveterans of comparable ages; in the depths of the 1890s depression, nearly 1 in 1,000 resident veterans died by suicide. This phenomenon finally drew attention when a newspaper article noted that a GAR officer and four other members of the same infantry company had committed suicide in 1895. But observers pursued the issue no farther.[21]

---

[20] Veteran population in Table 5.3 estimated as described in the appendix; civilian population from federal and state censuses, using age ranges corresponding to those of veterans.

[21] *Boston Herald,* July 7, 1895.

Journalists and their readers were hardly unaware of group tendencies in suicide. Newspapers published summaries of ethnic groups' suicidal behavior, sermons on self-destructive proclivities, and social scientists' latest analyses of suicide differentials by marital status, nationality, religion, and (current) military service. Those interested in authoritative explanations of suicide propensities could find "cosmic, ethnic, social, and biological influences" laid out in popular magazines.[22]

Nor was the public unacquainted with individual veterans' circumstances of suicide. The report of Andrew Perkins's death concluded that war-related "sickness and suffering undoubtedly led him to commit the act." William Ayers's hanging in 1890 was attributed to his being "unsettled in mind, owing to a sunstroke received while a soldier in the Rebellion." Frederick Morey "never fully recovered" from a wound at the Battle of the Wilderness. "It is believed that his ailments had made him temporarily insane" when Morey hanged himself in 1900.[23]

Analysts nonetheless ignored veterans as a meaningful group and no general alarum emerged from their suicides, perhaps because Gilded Age suicide publicity was as

---

[22] On group tendencies, see, e.g., *Springfield Republican*, June 13, 1871; *Boston Journal*, Aug. 20, 1900, Jan. 27, 1882; William Mathews, "Civilization and Suicide," *North American Review* 152 (1891), 470–485.

[23] *Boston Herald*, Mar. 21,1879; *Boston Journal*, Sept. 4, 1890; *Springfield Republican*, July 20, 1900.

shallow as it was broad. Published identification of suicidal veterans depended on relatives and acquaintances of the deceased, plus groups such as the GAR that assisted with funerals. Though the GAR accorded full military honors to members who took their own lives, other informants were evidently reluctant to link service and suicide: just over one-fourth of non-GAR veterans whose suicides appeared in Massachusetts newspapers were credited with their service.[24]

This reticence ensured that for every Andrew Perkins or William Ayers there would be at least one Harrison Horr or Edson Angier. Horr was the veteran introduced in Chapter 4 whose friendly-fire tragedy apparently haunted him until his suicide in 1876. The published report of his death, however, conveyed none of this. Horr's service went unmentioned, and he was said only to be "tired of life, and probably a little insane." Angier, a sergeant in the 35th Massachusetts Infantry, was pensioned for a hernia and a shoulder wound received at the Battle of the Crater. Seeking an increase in 1885, Angier complained that his disabilities had "laid [him] up about every year during the last ten years and [he] is unable to do the amount of labor he ought to do." Neither

---

[24] On the GAR's role in funerals, see McConnell, *Glorious Contentment*, 131–134; Gannon, *Won Cause*, 109–110. In the years covered by Table 5.3, 108 Union veterans' suicides were reported in Massachusetts newspapers; 19 were GAR members, and 24 others, or 27 percent of the nonmembers, were identified as veterans.

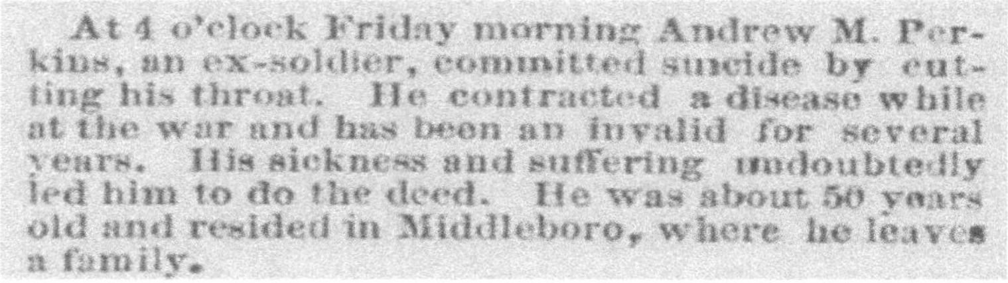

At 4 o'clock Friday morning Andrew M. Perkins, an ex-soldier, committed suicide by cutting his throat. He contracted a disease while at the war and has been an invalid for several years. His sickness and suffering undoubtedly led him to do the deed. He was about 50 years old and resided in Middleboro, where he leaves a family.

(a)

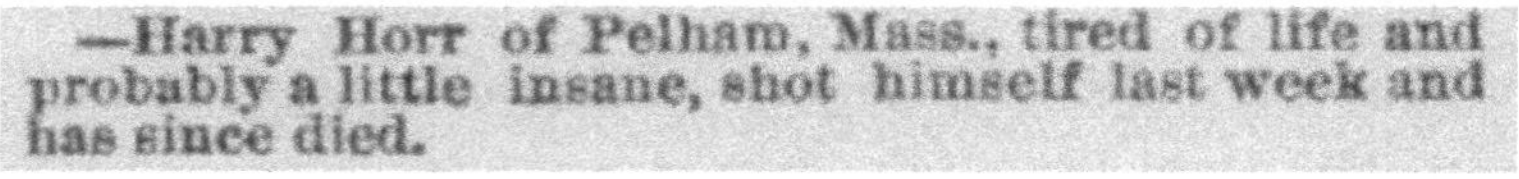

—Harry Horr of Pelham, Mass., tired of life and probably a little insane, shot himself last week and has since died.

(b)

Figure 5.3. (a) Newspapers occasionally connected suicides with Civil War service. *Boston Post*, March 22, 1879. (b) Former Pvt. Harrison Horr's death, however, illustrates news reports' more common practice of overlooking veterans' service and connections with their suicides. *Boston Post*, October 5, 1876

his service nor his disabilities were disclosed when Angier hanged himself in 1893. He was, according to the newspaper, a shoemaker "at work as usual" one day and dead the next, and "no cause is assigned for the act." When with hindsight we marvel that people in the Gilded Age failed to ask why so many veterans were dying by suicide, Horr's and Angier's cases suggest a response – with most veterans unidentified, the number of ex-soldiers committing suicide would hardly have appeared alarming (Figure 5.3).[25]

---

[25] *Springfield Republican*, Oct. 4, 1876; Surgeon's Certificate, July 22, 1885, Pension File of Edson J. Angier, 35th Massachusetts Infantry, RG 15, National Archives; *Boston Journal*, Mar. 25, 1893.

Driven to Suicide?

If veterans' suicide toll was not a contemporary question, we can convert it into a historical query. Why did Union veterans' suicide rate remain considerably above that for civilians through middle age?

Veterans' unique health problems are an obvious suspect. We have seen the contribution of wounds and disease to the suicides of veterans such as Perkins and Morey, but can the war's consequences be disentangled from the effects of aging? Amputations and head wounds command disproportionate attention in speculations about Civil War veterans' psychological illnesses. Amputations were the war's signature physical disability, and head wounds are clues to understanding mental disturbances. Both conditions are readily found among suicide accounts. James Forrest, whom we encountered in Chapter 1, typifies the ex-soldier driven to suicide by an amputation; Ira Lucas, who served in the 112th New York Infantry, exemplifies the consequences of a head wound. Lucas's wound occurred in the siege of Petersburg, and a quarter-century later it still caused him a "great deal of headache pain" and "faintness dizziness and darkness" when he tried to work on his farm. Lucas hanged himself in 1904.[26]

But these men were far outnumbered by suicidal ex-soldiers with more quotidian disorders. Charles DeLong

[26] Surgeon's Certificate, Mar. 26, 1890, record of Ira H. Lucas, 112th New York Infantry, ID 1311204060, EI White Troops.

spoke for numerous veterans when he complained of rheumatism contracted during the war, causing him "great pain in back and hips" and leaving him unable to work "except as I ride." Moses Rehrig echoed others in citing a hernia and other disabilities – in 1890 he declared that he was a carpenter by trade but "cannot climb a ladder." Both men eventually hanged themselves.[27]

Yet civilians could likewise be driven to suicide by chronic diseases and injuries. The experience of pensioned veterans illustrates the extra dimension of misery inflicted by the hardships of war. Before pension requirements were liberalized in 1890, applicants were expected to have a disability that originated in their service. Pension recipients in this period invite contradictory expectations. On the one hand, their disabilities may have put them at a heightened risk of suicide; on the other hand, pensions conferred economic security, especially during the depression of the mid-1870s.

Table 5.3, comparing suicide rates for Massachusetts pensioners and nonpensioned veterans at four observation years, indicates that the health effect prevailed. Though nonpensioners' suicide rate was above those for civilians shown in Table 5.2, the rate for pensioned veterans was

---

[27] Surgeon's Certificate, Mar. 4, 1885, record of Charles D. DeLong, 14th Vermont Infantry, ID 601407024, EI White Troops; Surgeon's Certificate, June 18, 1890, record of Moses Rehrig, 28th Pennsylvania Infantry, ID 1402805071, EI White Troops.

Table 5.3. *Suicide rates for pensioners and nonpensioned Union veterans in Massachusetts, 1875, 1880, 1885, 1890*

	Suicides per 100,000
Pensioners	58.2
Nonpensioned veterans	36.8

highest of all. Disease, injury, and wounds had damaged soldiers far beyond the experience of most men in their twenties and thirties. Now, with the damage compounded by the infirmities of age, veterans with more damage were more likely to resort to suicide.[28]

A second contributor to veterans' suicides emerges from their alleged motives. For all their faults, reporters' attributions suggest the broad outlines of suicidal behavior. Table 5.4 compares veterans' and civilians' supposed motives for suicide in Massachusetts, divided into two periods – 1875, 1880, and 1885, when most veterans were under age 50, and 1890, 1895, and 1900, when the majority had passed that age.

The sharpest difference between veterans and civilians was in substance abuse in the earlier period: veterans had

[28] Veterans' receipt of pensions ascertained in Organization Index to United States Civil War and Later Pension Files, 1861–1917, National Archives Microfilm Publication T289, Genealogical Society of Utah. Table 5.4 is based on observations only through 1890 to avoid confounding effects of current disabilities pensionable after 1890.

Table 5.4. Suicide motives reported in the press, Massachusetts veterans and civilians of comparable age, 1875, 1880, 1885, 1890, 1895, 1900

Motive	1875, 1880, 1885		1890, 1895, 1900	
	Percentage civilians' reported motives	Percentage veterans' reported motives	Percentage civilians' reported motives	Percentage veterans' reported motives
Financial	20	19	20	21
Physical health	20	12	31	40
Mental illness	21	28	26	19
Intemperance	12	23	7	8
All others[a]	27	18	16	12
Total number of motives	128	43	127	52

[a] See Table 4.3 for other motives.

nearly twice civilians' proportion of suicides attributed to intemperance. This should come as no surprise to those familiar with veterans, or suicide, or alcoholism. The popular image of Civil War veterans was reflexively bound up with alcohol. Soldiers had, according to one officer, been "initiated into the Army upon whisky, had whisky forced into them by the surgeons as a 'prophylactic' before they were wounded or taken sick, and finally had whisky poured into them in hospital." "The tremendous consumption of alcohol in our Civil War," in the estimate of an army surgeon, produced a "huge crop of drunken veterans." Government benefits allegedly made matters worse. A newspaper article maintained that "a good many old soldiers will drink up and carouse away their pension money almost as soon as they get it," and alcohol availability and abuse were endlessly contentious issues for soldiers' homes.[29]

Alcohol has long been suspected as a culprit behind suicide. A nineteenth-century social scientist concluded that "the relations between alcoholism and suicide have been shown by so many up to this time...that we believe it to be hardly necessary to insist on the general import of the statistical figures." Alcohol abuse is likewise

[29] Report of the Board of Managers of the National Home for Disabled Volunteer Soldiers, House Misc. Doc. 45, 44th Cong., 2nd sess. (1876–1877), 11; William Clark, "Alcohol for Soldiers," *Army and Navy Register*, June 4, 1900; *Springfield Republican*, Mar. 10, 1895; Marten, *Sing Not War*, 100–120.

blamed for suicidal behavior among twenty-first-century veterans.[30]

Journalists and medical examiners did their best to foster the image of the drunken and self-destructive veteran. Charles Stearns, "a man of particularly intemperate habits," got "crazy drunk" and cut his throat after threatening his family. For a week in 1879, Sherburn Morey, a veteran of the 12th Massachusetts Infantry, "had taken no food but had been constantly drinking whiskey." After failing to asphyxiate himself, Morey died by a pistol shot. Thomas Faulkner, "a veteran soldier of intemperate habits," went on "a spree all the week" in Boston before cutting his throat. Joseph H. Goodwin was "a pensioner who came to Boston from Maine quarterly to draw his money, & spend it for liquor on a prolonged spree." Goodwin died of alcoholism in 1880.[31]

Investigators were less assiduous in probing beneath the surface of veterans' suicides. The fact of intoxication was enough, signaling a supposed deficiency of character that led

[30] Enrico Morselli, *Suicide: An Essay on Comparative Moral Statistics* (New York: Appleton, 1992), 288; Hyungjin Kim et al., "Predictors of Suicide in Patient Charts among Patients with Depression in the Veterans Administration Health System: Importance of Prescription Drug and Alcohol Abuse," *Journal of Clinical Psychiatry* 73 (2012), 1260–1275.

[31] *Boston Daily Advertiser*, Sept. 16, 1878; View of Body of Sherburn F. Morey, May 23, 1879; Thomas D. Faulkner, June 29, 1880; Joseph H. Goodwin, Sept. 15, 1880, Reports of Medical Examiners, Countway Library of Medicine, Harvard University.

logically to suicide. Though the medical establishment was edging toward acceptance of alcoholism as a disease, a body of opinion vigorously dissented. "Any ailment which can be cured by moral suasion, religious enthusiasm or simple will power can not be organic in origin," wrote one physician, accusing his colleagues of "fostering upon a credulous public the host of inebriates in this country." The typical alcoholic "was vicious before he learned to drink" and "never had any manhood about him." There was no place in this view for alcoholism driven by pain from war wounds, nor was there much mention of disabilities in news accounts of alcohol-related suicides. Charles Stearns's wound from the Battle of Fair Oaks went unremarked, as did the partial paralysis from a bullet still lodged in Sherburn Morey's chest; Thomas Faulkner's amputated arm and other injuries were noted in the newspaper but overlooked by a medical examiner.[32]

[32] W. C. Howle, "The Drink Habit," *Journal of the American Medical Association*, 19 (1892), 575; *Boston Journal*, May 23, 1879, June 30, 1880. Morey (no apparent relation to Frederick) was wounded at Spotsylvania and suffered from a urinary tract constriction. Pension File of Sherburne F. Morey, 12th Massachusetts Infantry, RG 15, National Archives. There is no extant newspaper report of Joseph Goodwin's death, and the medical examiner's report mentions no disability. On initial steps toward a disease view of alcoholism, see Mark E. Lender and James K. Martin, *Drinking in America: A History* (New York: Simon and Schuster, 1987), 119–122; on persisting views of alcohol abuse as moral degeneracy, see Marten, *Sing Not War*, 104–105.

Denial could not eliminate the connection. Alcohol-induced suicides, typically rooted in war injuries, exacerbated Massachusetts veterans' rate of suicide in the 1870s and 1880s. By the following decade, when most veterans were older than 50, such suicides had fallen to negligible levels for them and civilians alike. Deteriorating health itself had become the leading attributed motive for all middle-aged male suicides. Ill health was especially dominant among veterans, reaffirming its role in driving their suicides higher than the rate for civilians.[33]

"Most of the Boys Have Lost Their Purpose in Life"

If Union veterans were unusually suicidal, we might expect them to have been doubly so in soldiers' homes. The veterans' advocates, reformers, and politicians who shaped the

[33] Analysis of suicide motivations invites consideration of the "copycat effect," the assumption that suicidal behavior is suggestible and leads to clustering of deaths. For an overview, see Loren Coleman, *The Copycat Effect: How the Media and Popular Culture Trigger the Mayhem of Tomorrow's Headlines* (New York: Simon and Schuster, 2004); for a nineteenth-century example of clustering, see David Silkenat, *Moments of Despair: Suicide, Divorce, and Debt in Civil War Era North Carolina* (Chapel Hill: University of North Carolina Press, 2011), 59–61. An examination of late nineteenth-century Massachusetts, however, found no significant clusters of male suicides; see Larry M. Logue, "Elephants and Epistemology: Evidence of Suicide in the Gilded Age," *Journal of Social History* 49 (2015), 374–386. Veterans could have been an exception, but the scarce publicity given to suicides' military service renders this dubious.

federal home system never solved a conundrum at the heart of their mission. An early president of the system promised "to make the remaining years of the disabled soldiers happy and comfortable" by providing "the comforts of life, with means of occupation and amusement." Putting comfort ahead of employment may have been his recognition of a dilemma facing all residential institutions. Soldiers' homes offered residents paid employment and provided libraries, schools, and entertainment, but they could not eliminate boredom and its gateway to suicide. An official admitted that "these men who work for the Home are not working for their living...They are all provided for by the Home with everything that the ordinary laborer works for." A chaplain reported that "the complaints I hear are usually in regard to [residents'] having nothing to do; the time passes slowly."[34]

A resident at the home for regular army veterans in Washington, DC, explained the turn from boredom to suicide:

> Just the same thing day in and day out all the year round...How awfully tired a fellow gets of just eating three times a day and walking just so much and lying down and getting up and buttoning and unbuttoning. Most of the boys

[34] Annual Report of the Board of Managers of the National Home for Disabled Volunteer Soldiers, House Misc. Doc. 97, 43rd Cong., 2nd sess. (1874–1875), 3; Investigation of the National Home for Disabled Volunteer Soldiers, House Rpt. 2676, 48th Cong., 2nd sess. (1884–1885), 651, 573.

have lost their purpose in life; and many suffer from old wounds, but the great trouble, sir, is the sameness, every fellow feeling that he has nothing to look forward to. He's provided for, and that's all. Say what you will, sir, there's no wanting like the wanting of a man who doesn't know what he wants and does know there's never a chance to get it.

The surgeon at the Ohio federal home declared that under the prior administration "we had a good many suicides, seven, eight, or ten a year. I think it was as much from men sitting idly there, having nothing to do, as anything else." If accurate, his assertion would imply a rate of 200 to 300 suicides per 100,000 residents. A disaffected resident expanded the arraignment: "petty persecution" over minor infractions had "caused men to commit suicide. I know this to be a fact, because I know my own feelings, and I can judge others by those." These were institutions in which purposelessness and oppression allegedly conduced to suicidal despair (Figure 5.4).[35]

The institutional records are less damning. The surgeon exaggerated the number of suicides at the Ohio home – officials recorded no more than two suicides annually in the years before his tenure. The suicide rate for the federal system as a whole from 1875 to 1900 was 42 per 100,000, lower than most of the rates for veterans shown in Table 5.3. We might add men such as Thomas Faulkner, who left the

[35] "All the Year Round" (syndicated report), *Hamilton* [Ohio] *Journal*, July 21, 1894; Investigation of the National Home, 153, 264.

Figure 5.4. Images from the Central Branch of the National Home for Disabled Volunteer Soldiers, Dayton, Ohio. The federal homes provided employment, recreation, and manicured grounds, but some observers believed that the daily routine contributed to residents' suicides. From Dayton Veterans Administration Archives

federal home in Maine just before he hanged himself in Boston. Cases such as Faulkner's were too infrequent, however, to raise the homes' suicide rate to the toll for Massachusetts veterans.[36]

The fate of James Forbes and John Meighan offers a counterpoint to the depiction of soldiers' homes. Neither veteran resided in the homes, and both knew what they wanted. Forbes, an unemployed machinist living in Connecticut, returned from his latest search for work "penniless and despondent," and he "did not know what he should do." He told his wife that he "had come home to die" and took an overdose of laudanum. Meighan was a New Jersey contractor whose business failed in the early 1890s. He moved in with his daughters after his wife's death, but "dependence made him despondent." Meighan was heard to say that "he didn't think he would live long in his poverty-stricken condition" shortly before he drowned himself in the Hudson River.[37]

---

[36] Suicide rate calculated from average yearly population and suicides reported for each branch from 1875 through 1900, in Annual Reports of the Board of Managers of the National Home for Disabled Volunteer Soldiers, House Misc. Docs., 44th through 56th Cong. It is of course possible that suicides were underreported by NHDVS officials. Newspaper reports are the most effective check on reporting accuracy (see Chapter 2); a sampling of newspapers from a number of cities found occasional reports of suicides at federal soldiers' homes, all of which were acknowledged in the homes' registers.

[37] *New Haven Reporter*, Jan. 15, 1889; *New York Times*, Mar. 25, 1893; *New York World,* Mar. 24, 1893.

Rather than raising suicidal despair to unequaled levels, soldiers' homes substituted one source of despondency for another. They imposed monotony and intrusive discipline, but they also lightened the burden of subsistence that accounted for the deaths of Forbes and Meighan and as many as one in five of all veterans' suicides. The rough equivalence of suicide rates in and out of the homes points to broader forces shaping veterans' fatal decisions.

Old Age in the New Century

The popular conception of the troubled veteran imagines a young ex-soldier with a severe physical disability or traumatic memories. Aged veterans are depicted as those who escaped these afflictions, now rocking on a porch and reliving their glory days. Neither of these images squares with the circumstances of Charles Cole in the early twentieth century. According to his physician, the 72-year-old Cole "sat in his chair day and night, and was unable to assume a recumbent position." Then, "worn out by continued suffering," Cole had attempted suicide by shooting himself and cutting his throat. Nor do the images match the later life of Henry Young, who "talks only after his suspicions are allayed by sympathetic & kindly persuasion," whereupon he "cries & tears flow freely when he tells of being persecuted" and indicated that he "wants to die to be rid of imaginary troubles" (Figure 5.5).[38]

SURGEON'S CERTIFICATE.

Chas. M. Cole

Company G, 28 Reg't 111. Vol. Inf.

Indianola, Vermilion Co., Ill.

Address of Board. { Danville, _____ P. O.

111inois. _____ State.

December 26, 1907. , 190

[Date of examination.]

Rheumatism, disease of heart and lungs.

_____. He receives a pension of __Twenty-four__ dollars per month. He makes the following statement in regard to the origin of his disabilities and date when first discovered by him: Contracted rheumatism, disease of heart and lungs on the Missippi River during the sergice. For two years has he been an invalid by reasons of these disabilities mentioned, and can no t perform any manual labor.

Birthplace, ____Penna____ ; age, 72 ____ years; height, 5' 1d 1-; weight, __124 1-2__ pounds; complexion, light ____ ; color of eyes, __blue__ ___; color of hair, __gray__ ; occupation armer ____ ; permanent marks and scars other than those described below, _____

We hereby certify that upon examination we find the following objective conditions:
Pulse rate, 118 _____ ; respiration, __34__ _____ ; temperature, 98.0 ____ ;
[Sitting, standing, after exercise.] _____ [Sitting, standing, after exercise.]

Rheumatism.- All the digital articulations are more or less enlarged and limited in motion. Both knee-joints are enlarged, and the claimant stands and walks with the legs in se semi-flexion. The nates are markedly atrophied. The right shoulder is sensitive, grates and is limited in motion 1-2. For rheumatism, we rate, 14-18.

Heart.- The apex-beat is in the 6th interspace and one half inch to the left of the nipple-line. The impulse is feeble and the rhythm disordered. Auscultation shows d ouble murmur at the mitral orifice. Dyspnoea is marked and the legs are oedematous; the skin is cold and cyanotic. The dyspnoea is so great that he can exercise but little. For five months, this claimant sat in his chair day and night, and was unable to assume a recumbent position. Worn out by continued suffering and distressing dyspnoea, the claimant attempted suicide about six weeks ago by shooting himself in the head and inflictkng a knife wound of the neck. The wound of head is subcutaneous and the missile did not enter the cranial cavity. The wound of neck severed an important bloodvessel and the claimant was exsanguinated by the loss of blood. The hemorrhage resulting from these self inflicted wounds relieved the pulmonary stasis and its consequent dyspnoea, and it appears that this man can now lie down at night and enjoy some rest. The oedematous cond

Figure 5.5. Surgeon's certificate from pension examination of Charles Cole, describing his suicide attempt in 1907. Record Group 15, National Archives

As we follow veterans such as Cole and Young into a new century, we are confronted by a question. Were their psychological problems legacies of the Civil War, or were they men with a mental illness who happened to be veterans? The evidence at first points to the latter conclusion. Veterans of both races tried to link mental illnesses to their service, but the Pension Bureau usually rejected the connection. Cole claimed that his problems began when he contracted rheumatism near the war's end, Young cited service-related diarrhea, and Scott Alexander, a 67-year-old African American, blamed a wound for making him "so nervous I cant feed myself." Officials approved payments for their physical disabilities, but included nothing for service-connected nervous disorders. Veterans' statements tying psychological problems to the war were often treated as claim-agent-orchestrated ploys for increased pensions.[39]

Yet there is more in the pension records. Efforts to extract "objective truth" from pension claims will frequently

[38] Surgeon's Certificate, Dec. 26, 1907, Pension File of Charles M. Cole, 28th Illinois Infantry, RG 15, National Archives (Cole's suicide attempts failed, and he died of heart disease in 1908); Surgeon's Certificate, Sept. 21, 1899, Pension File of Henry Young, 83rd Illinois Infantry, RG 15, National Archives.

[39] Surgeon's Certificate, June 16, 1909, record of Scott Alexander, 17th US Colored Infantry, ID 9001701203, EI Colored Troops II (see the appendix for full citations of EI samples); Decision on Increased Pension, Mar. 20, 1908, Cole Pension File; Decision on Increased Pension, Apr. 24, 1900, Young Pension File ("insanity not a result").

encounter contradictory testimony and selective official interpretations. There is no denying, however, that applying for a service-connected disability pension vivified veterans' recollections of the Civil War. Pension laws held open the possibility that the war's aftereffects could persist into old age, and numerous veterans responded. When Charles Cole declared that he had suffered from "disease of lungs since April 1865 caused by falling in Mississippi River," and Scott Alexander pointed out that "I was shot in the Battle of Nashville," they were reliving their war as surely as were ex-soldiers moved by nostalgia. Of course the two forms of reexperiencing were not identical. Recollections by Alexander and the others sprang from pain rather than satisfaction, and their remembering was private in contrast to other veterans' public recounting of wartime deeds. Cole, Young, and Alexander demonstrate the delayed onset of psychological disorders in some veterans. The origin could be as mundane as a transportation mishap or an everyday disease, but these risks define warfare as much as do shot and shell. It is difficult to explain the psychological distress of these veterans, and others like them, without invoking their wartime service.[40]

[40] Surgeon's Certificate, June 12, 1908, Cole Pension File; Surgeon's Certificate, June 16, 1909, Scott Alexander record. Contradictory testimony about Young's mental illness is apparent in Affidavit of Theodore Bradley, June 1, 1882, and E. W. Zook to Pension Bureau, May 15, 1923, Young Pension File.

Aging and Fatal Decisions

When they died by suicide, older veterans' ordeals became public occurrences. Since nearly all veterans who lived past 1900 received a pension under liberalized provisions, the EI samples, with their reliance on pension records, provide better information for them than for younger ex-soldiers. The sample of post-1900 suicides is too small for comparison with civilian rates, but the pension records point to the context and motivation of suicides.[41]

---

[41] An estimated three-quarters of surviving soldiers had pensions in 1900, increasing to 90 percent in 1910; see Theda Skocpol, *Protecting Soldiers and Mothers: The Political Origins of Social Policy in the United States* (Cambridge, MA: Harvard University Press, 1992), 108–109. The appropriate benchmark for suicide rates would be suicides among older men in the "registration states" from which the Census Bureau collected mortality data in the late nineteenth and early twentieth centuries; for a detailed description of the registration system, see US Census Office, *Mortality Statistics, 1900 to 1904* (Washington, DC: Government Printing Office, 1906), ix–xvii. The number of these states (plus selected cities in other states) expanded from 11 in 1900 to 35 in 1920 (including the District of Columbia in both cases). There are too few suicides in the EI samples in a given year to compare them directly to the Census Bureau's yearly reports. If the EI samples' suicides and person-years are aggregated from 1900 to 1920, the result is one state (New York) with a high suicide rate of 65.3 per 100,000 person-years, but also seven states from the 1900 registration area with no suicides; the resulting rates of zero obviate comparison with the Census Bureau's statistics, which are aggregated for all registration states. The Census Bureau declined to report population totals

Older veterans' deaths underscore the tenuous connection between suicide and nineteenth-century conceptions of mental illness. Henry Young's case is instructive. The Pension Bureau required examining physicians to report any "suicidal disposition" they found, which they did when informed that Young had attempted to kill himself. The physicians were also informed that Young was currently an insane asylum inmate, which undoubtedly influenced their perspective and should influence ours. Institutionalization and suicide were intertwined: attempted suicide could be cause for a commitment, and confinement could lead to suicide. Half of the Union veterans in a sample of Indiana asylum inmates were diagnosed with or acted on suicidal impulses.[42]

---

by age for the 1900 registration area (see Census Office, *Mortality Statistics,* xviii), but New York's EI sample suicide rate can be compared to 61.5 for all men age 65 and older in 1910 and 46.6 for 1920; see US Census Office, *Mortality Rates, 1910–1920* (Washington, DC: Government Printing Office, 1922), 625. Massachusetts, whose superior death records were used in previous chapters to compare veterans' and civilians' suicide rates, began to abandon the readily perusable death registers after 1900 in favor of individual death certificates, making the search for veterans' suicides impracticable.

[42] US Pension Office, *Instructions to Examining Surgeons for Pensions* (Washington, DC: Government Printing Office, 1893), 13; Surgeon's Certificate, Sept. 21, 1899, Young Pension File; Gerald N. Grob, *The Mad among Us: A History of the Care of America's Mentally Ill* (New York: Free Press, 1994), 80–81; Dean, *Shook over Hell,* 151.

From the perspective of the larger veteran population, however, the link between suicide and diagnosed insanity all but disappears. None of the EI sample members who died by suicide had been committed to asylums, and only one was judged by examining physicians to be suicidal. Physicians duly noted Charles Cole's suicide attempt, but they treated the incident differently from the evaluation of Henry Young. Cole had never been in an insane asylum, and physicians said nothing in his examinations about insanity. Cole's attempt to kill himself was treated as a release from protracted suffering rather than the nadir of a psychological decline.

Apart from the prior attempt, most of the suicidal veterans in the EI samples shared Cole's plight. Their final pension examinations, sometimes within months of their death, reveal an accumulation of debilitating conditions. A few months before he shot himself at age 62, John Hanson complained of rheumatism, impaired vision, and heart disease. Prior to his suicide in 1906, Andrew Powell reported "pain stiffness contraction of tendons shortness of breath cough weakness sleeplessness." Three years before his asphyxiation, Pierre Pettit described "lameness and pain" in his arm and leg, impaired vision and hearing, and urinary problems. After describing various conditions in previous sessions, a few despondent veterans made their last examination statement the equivalent of a suicide note. Oliver Case's statement declared that he was "not able to perform any manual [labor] for about 15 years," and Allen Green, a veteran of the 19th Colored Infantry, complained a month before his suicide that he was "feeble from age and cannot work." Unlike distinctive causes such as failed relationships and alcoholism that had impelled younger comrades to suicide, the common infirmities of old age dominated Union veterans' fatal decisions in the twentieth century.[43]

War's Deep Reach

Surviving the initial postwar years provided little insurance against later misery. Physical and mental disabilities were conjoined: the Gilded Age had few reconstructive treatments for wounds and few remedies for conditions such as chronic diarrhea, so physical maladies frequently shaded into mental illness. Veterans and their families were loath to confess psychological problems to census-takers, but pension physicians could not help noticing symptoms of mental illness in numerous middle-aged applicants. Some committed suicide,

[43] Surgeon's Certificate, Jan. 21, 1903, record of John W. Hanson, 87th Illinois Infantry, ID 2108703049, EI White Troops; Surgeon's Certificate, Apr. 4, 1906, record of Andrew J. Powell, 91st Ohio Infantry, ID 2409105108, EI White Troops; Surgeon's Certificate, Mar. 8, 1906, record of Pierre Pettit, 10th New York Infantry, ID 1301004077, EI White Troops; Surgeon's Certificate, Jan. 15, 1902, record of Oliver W. Case, 65th Illinois Infantry, ID 2106505016, EI White Troops; Surgeon's Certificate, Nov. 17, 1906, record of Allen Green, 19th US Colored Infantry, ID 9001909223, EI Colored Troops I.

but the relationship between mental illness diagnoses and suicide was only vaguely understood. The elevated risk of suicide among veterans pensioned for wartime disabilities, and the high rate for all veterans compared to civilian men, are our clearest evidence of the Civil War's deep reach into the lives of ex-soldiers.

6

Trials of Black Veterans

The preceding chapters' discussions have pertained mostly to white Union veterans. Their plight is a backdrop for similar consideration of African American ex-soldiers. As intense as the Civil War was for white soldiers, their experience may have been eclipsed by that of the African American regiments. No white soldiers shared the trials of George Bryant, who was captured near Petersburg in 1864 and sold into slavery. No whites were murdered because of their skin color in the manner of victims at Fort Pillow, Tennessee, Poison Spring, Arkansas, and other places.[1]

---

[1] Affidavit of Jan. 31, 1876, record of George Bryant, 23rd US Colored Infantry, ID 9002306136, EI Colored Troops II. On massacres of black soldiers, see John Cimprich, *Fort Pillow, a Civil War*

We have promoted pension files and soldiers' home records as rich sources for exploring posttraumatic stress, but African American veterans pose a distinctive challenge. Both kinds of evidence are back-loaded – accelerating participation produced a majority of records long after the war's end – but the disproportion is especially pronounced among black veterans. Their units were organized later and saw less combat than did white ones, so African Americans had fewer of the battle wounds that essentially guaranteed a federal pension in the system's early years. Black veterans were less than half as likely as whites to apply for a war-related pension; when the wartime restriction was relaxed in 1890, African Americans' pension-seeking surged to match that of white veterans.[2]

Massacre, and Public Memory (Baton Rouge: Louisiana State University Press, 2011); Mark K. Christ, ed., *"All Cut to Pieces and Gone to Hell": The Civil War, Race Relations, and the Battle of Poison Spring* (Little Rock, AR: August House, 2003); Thomas D. Mays, "The Battle of Saltville," in John David Smith, ed., *Black Soldiers in Blue: African American Troops in the Civil War Era* (Chapel Hill: University of North Carolina Press, 2002), 200–226; J. Matthew Gallman, "In Your Hands That Musket Means Liberty: African American Soldiers and the Battle of Olustee," in Joan Waugh and Gary W. Gallagher, eds., *Wars within a War: Controversy and Conflict over the American Civil War* (Chapel Hill: University of North Carolina Press, 2009), 87–108.

[2] Larry M. Logue and Peter Blanck found that 20 percent of black veterans applied for a new pension before 1890, versus 44 percent of whites; more than 90 percent of surviving veterans of both

African Americans also shied away from soldiers' homes. Federal home residents from the US Colored Troops never matched their share of the wartime army. These tendencies created a bias in the records of black veterans, underrepresenting those who died before federal benefits were liberalized. The bias poses a particular difficulty for the EI samples, whose information depends heavily on pension records. Our assessment of psychological stress among black veterans will address the challenge in two ways. To compensate for the shortage of early pension records, we will seek evidence of postwar distress in other sources. When we use the EI sample and its extensive evidence on veterans' later lives, we will make allowances for African Americans' distinctive pension-seeking.[3]

---

races applied after 1890. Logue and Blanck, *Race, Ethnicity, and Disability: Veterans and Benefits in Post–Civil War America* (New York: Cambridge University Press, 2010), 47–55. Donald R. Shaffer argues that poverty and illiteracy were largely to blame for lower African American application rates, especially among slaves. Shaffer, *After the Glory: The Struggles of Black Civil War Veterans* (Lawrence: University Press of Kansas, 2004), 122–125. This argument carries less weight in light of the post-1890 surge in applications.

[3] On African Americans in soldiers' homes, see Shaffer, *After the Glory*, 137–142; Logue and Blanck, *Race, Ethnicity, and Disability*, 130–141; Patrick Kelly, *Creating a National Home: Building the Veterans' Welfare State, 1865–1900* (Cambridge, MA: Harvard University Press, 1997), 98–99.

Clashing Views of African American Insanity

If contemporaries showed minimal concern about the traumas of white veterans, they evinced none at all for African Americans. Black veterans were not so much ignored, however, as subsumed in a general discussion of African Americans' mental health. The discourse included a few experts who held that African Americans were less prone to mental illness than were whites. George Beard, originator of the neurasthenia diagnosis discussed in Chapter 5, was a devotee of the doctrine that civilization bred insanity. Beard had visited former slaves in the southeastern Sea Islands, "who at no time have been brought into relation to our civilization, except insofar as it is exhibited in a very few white individuals." Maintaining that "these thousands of negroes are types of negroes all over the South," he concluded that "there is almost no insanity among these negroes; there is no functional nervous disease or symptoms among them of any name or phase." Frederick Hoffman, a statistician who acknowledged the shortcomings of available information, likewise found that "insanity and lunacy are less common among the colored population than among the whites."[4]

---

[4] Beard allowed that insanity may have "somewhat increased" in large cities. George M. Beard, *American Nervousness, Its Causes and Consequences* (New York: G. P. Putnam, 1881), 188, 190, 189; Frederick L. Hoffman, "Race Traits and Tendencies of the American Negro," *Publications of the American Economic Association* 11 (1896), 126. See also Martin Summers, "'Suitable Care of the African

These observers were drowned out by southern asylum administrators. Ignoring comparisons with whites, these men warned that emancipation had unleashed an epidemic of African American insanity. According to the head of Georgia's asylum, "freedom removed all hygienic restraints and [former slaves] were no longer obedient to the inexorable laws of health, plunging into all sorts of excesses and vices." They had "developed a highly insane, consumptive, syphilitic and alcoholic constitution which predisposes them to diseases which formerly they were free from." The typical slave had "spent his quiet, humble life in his little log cabin, with his master to care for every want of self and family," wrote a North Carolina asylum superintendent. Then, "without preparation of any sort, the new negro was invested with the highest functions of citizenship before the healing of the marks of the chains that had bound him." The predictable result was "a beautiful harvest of mental and physical degeneration." "Prior to the late civil war, a crazy negro was an unwonted sight," declared the head of the St. Louis asylum. "Now, the asylums of the South teem with them, and the tendency to insanity in the race is steadily and rapidly increasing."[5]

When Afflicted with Insanity': Race, Madness, and Social Order in Comparative Perspective," *Bulletin of the History of Medicine* 84 (2010), 58–91.
[5] Theophilus O. Powell, "The Increase of Insanity and Tuberculosis in the Southern Negro since 1860," *Journal of the American Medical Association* 26 (1896), 1186, 1185; J. F. Miller, "The Effects of

These assertions are polemics and not evidence, but they serve useful purposes. Together with the assertions of Beard and Hoffman, they demonstrate that widely diverging opinions on African Americans' mental health could agree in overlooking black veterans. The omission may have been the product of numbers. In the only report of its kind, the 1890 census identified a total of 73 "insane" black veterans in the United States, only six of whom lived in the South. But the oversight was as likely the result of collective denial. Northern writers and commemoration organizers, more interested in reconciliation than in veracity, minimized the contributions of black soldiers. Southern writers could bring themselves to mention black troops only when they insisted that "the employment, as soldiers, against the Confederacy, of this immense number of blacks, was a brutality and crime in sight of the world." When men's soldiering had no legitimate purpose, worrying about their posttraumatic stress was pointless.[6]

Emancipation upon the Mental and Physical Health of the Negro of the South," *North Carolina Medical Journal* 38 (1896), 289, 292, 290; Annual Report of the Superintendent of the St. Louis Insane Asylum, *Mayor's Message with Accompanying Documents to the Municipal Assembly of the City of Saint Louis* (St. Louis, MO: Nixon-Jones, 1887), 229.

[6] US Census Office, *Report on the Insane, Feeble-Minded, Deaf and Dumb, and Blind in the United States at the Eleventh Census* (Washington, DC: Government Printing Office, 1895), 236; E. A. Pollard, *Southern History of the War* (New York: Charles R. Richardson, 1866), 196. On devaluing black soldiers' role in public memory, see

Black veterans knew better. They knew that they had won the admiration of their officers during the war and that they were held in high esteem by their peers afterward. "Free and bond men came and sacrificed their lives upon the altar of freedom for the liberty that you and I enjoy," declared a Grand Army of the Republic chaplain, celebrating "the dark-skinned heroes [who] fell with face to the foe and achieved glorious victories in defense of the American flag."[7]

But the horrors of war had threatened all who served. We need not accept the generalizations of asylum managers to wonder about the psychological effects of warfare on men who had grown up as slaves. The hardships of slavery may have made soldiers more vulnerable to the traumas of

---

Shaffer, *After the Glory*, 174–177, 179–193; David W. Blight, *Race and Reunion: The Civil War in American Memory* (Cambridge, MA: Harvard University Press, 2001); Joseph Glatthaar, *Forged in Battle: The Civil War Alliance of Black Soldiers and White Officers* (New York: Free Press, 1990), 260–261, 263–264. On countervailing efforts to credit the black role, see Barbara A. Gannon, *The Won Cause: Black and White Comradeship in the Grand Army of the Republic* (Chapel Hill: University of North Carolina Press, 2011); Glatthaar, *Forged in Battle,* 257–259.

[7] *Christian Recorder*, Jan. 28, 1886. See also Shaffer, *After the Glory*, 177–179; Caroline E. Janney, *Remembering the Civil War: Reunion and the Limits of Reconciliation* (Chapel Hill: University of North Carolina Press, 2013); Glatthaar, *Forged in Battle*, 257–259; Richard Reid, *Freedom for Themselves: North Carolina's Black Soldiers in the Civil War Era* (Chapel Hill: University of North Carolina Press, 2012), 311–315.

campaigning and combat, or the act of escaping from slavery and fighting for its eradication might have conferred a resistance to those traumas. Using evidence produced by the nineteenth century's understanding of mental disorders, we will explore the psychological trials of slaves and freeborn black men who had been to war.

Race and the Experience of Mental Illness

Our exploration begins with glimpses of wartime origins. Army surgeons reported their diagnoses on forms later compiled in the *Medical and Surgical History of the Civil War.* Officials recognized several nervous disorders, of which "insanity" best approaches our interest in war's traumas. The *Medical and Surgical History*'s tables on the US Colored Troops contain the two years, mid-1863 through mid-1865, that saw the full inclusion of African American soldiers; the equitable basis for comparison is whites' diagnoses in the two years of their own introduction to the war.[8]

Soldiers' tabulated disorders show a modest contrast between the races: whites were diagnosed with 14.8 cases of insanity per 10,000 soldier-years in their inaugural period, while African Americans presented 12.1 cases per 10,000 in their first two years. The *Medical and Surgical History* provides little beyond these aggregate statistics; no finer

---

[8] *Medical and Surgical History of the War of the Rebellion*, 6 vols. (Washington, DC: Government Printing Office, 1870–1888), I: 638–639, 711 (hereafter cited as *MSH*).

categories of insanity are presented, and no distinction is made between freeborn black soldiers and former slaves.[9]

The records of the Government Hospital for the Insane in Washington, DC, offer details on some of the men with nervous disorders (Figure 6.1). Army regulations required intractable cases of insanity to be committed to the

---

[9] On insanity as understood during the Civil War, see Eric T. Dean Jr., *Shook over Hell: Post-Traumatic Stress, Vietnam, and the Civil War* (Cambridge, MA: Harvard University Press, 1997), 116–127. The *MSH* also reports epilepsy, sunstroke, and nostalgia as nervous disorders. As noted earlier, we have excluded epilepsy. We likewise exclude sunstroke as an additional condition that has substantial differences from the primarily psychological disorders that are this book's focus; on sunstroke in the Civil War, see *MSH*, V, 853–860. Recent studies have argued that nostalgia, though it displayed a correspondence with our understanding of posttraumatic stress, was actually a distinctive condition arising from severed connections with home and family. Frances Clarke, "So Lonesome I Could Die: Nostalgia and Debates over Emotional Control in the Civil War North," *Journal of Social History* 41 (2007), 253–282; David Anderson, "Dying of Nostalgia: Homesickness in the Union Army during the Civil War," *Civil War History* 56 (2010), 247–282. The rates cited in this paragraph are based on soldier-years because *MSH* tabulates the average monthly strength of Union forces each year. See also B. Christopher Frueh and Jeffrey A. Smith, "Suicide, Alcoholism, and Psychiatric Illness among Union Forces during the US Civil War," *Journal of Anxiety Disorders* 26 (2012), 769–775, who suggest that the psychological disorder rates in *MSH* are remarkably low. It must be borne in mind, however, that *MSH* rates are "period" rates based on soldier-years rather than the potentially greater cumulative individual probability of disorders and that they are physicians' diagnoses rather than the self-reported conditions that are typical in analyses in our own time.

Figure 6.1. (a) The main building of the Government Hospital for the Insane (later known as St. Elizabeths). The Hospital was the main care facility for active-duty service members and soldiers' home residents with mental illnesses. (House Doc. 5, 55th Cong., 3rd sess.). (b) The Hospital for the Insane segregated patients by race, reserving the West Lodge for African-American men. (RG 418-G331, National Archives)

Government Hospital in lieu of a discharge. The admission records of the Government Hospital list 27 black soldiers.[10]

---

[10] St. Elizabeths Hospital, Register of Cases, RG 418, National Archives (hereafter cited as GHI Register). St. Elizabeths was formerly the Government Hospital for the Insane.

Half of these men were former slaves. Lower than the slave proportion in the army as a whole, their number gives no comfort to the contention that freedom bred insanity. Four of the insanity cases involved wounds, the most serious of which disabled Joseph Lacy and Samuel Bird during the campaign for Petersburg, Virginia, in 1864. Lacy was shot in the hip; the site was "still suppurating" two months later, undoubtedly contributing to the insanity that "at any moment [may] endanger the lives of the surrounding patients." Bird's arm wound was equally severe. An army surgeon declared that Bird "showed no symptoms of Insanity until after he suffered amputation of arm."[11]

Three instances of insanity supposedly predated the war. William Hampton was hospitalized for various ailments during the siege of Petersburg and later in Brownsville, Texas. A final confinement resulted in a diagnosis of "periodical

[11] The US army did not formally collect statistics on former servitude, but 22 of the 27 insanity cases are classifiable based on occasional notations in military records and owners' claims for compensation for losing their slaves. More than 80 percent of enlisted men in the US Colored Troops came from slave states; see Ira Berlin, Joseph F. Reidy, and Leslie S. Rowland, eds., *Freedom: A Documentary History of Emancipation* (New York: Cambridge University Press, 1982), ser. II, *The Black Military Experience*, 12. Quotations from H. R. Curtis to G. W. Blake, Dec. 17, 1864, Service Record of Joseph Lacy, 4th US Colored Infantry, Civil War Compiled Service Records, RG 94, National Archives (hereafter cited as Compiled Service Records); D. L. Huntington to Adjutant General, Dec. 14, 1865, Service Record of Samuel Bird (alias Joseph Carpenter), 43rd US Colored Infantry, Compiled Service Records.

insanity ... existing previous to enlistment." Byron Miles's "unsound mind," in the opinion of a regimental surgeon, "existed long anterior to his enlistment." Henry Endicott was allegedly "subject to [insane] spells since childhood." The army sent Hampton to the Government Hospital and discharged Miles and Endicott.[12]

The remaining soldiers had less amply documented causes for their conditions, but they contributed to two distinctive patterns. Nine of the insanity cases occurred among African Americans serving as occupation forces in the South. Sent to postings as distant as Florida and Texas, black soldiers found resentment of occupiers compounded by racial animosity. Whites in Columbus, Georgia, "had never seen any colored soldiers in their midst, they considered it an insult, a disgrace to them, and all possible means were employed to get rid of the garrison." Black soldiers' assertions of their rights as men were repaid with threats of violence. A former Confederate vowed that "*if a nigger insults*

---

[12] Certificate of Insanity, July 27, 1865, Service Record of William Hampton, 9th US Colored Infantry, Compiled Service Records; Discharge Certificate, Service Record of Byron Miles, 26th US Colored Infantry, Compiled Service Records.; G. M. Pease, request for admission to GHI, April 4, 1864, and Discharge Certificate, Service Record of Henry C. Endicott, 54th Massachusetts Colored Infantry, Compiled Service Records. Army officials were not supposed to discharge soldiers for insanity, but Miles's discharge referred to "his being mentally unfit to direct his own actions." Endicott was meant to be sent to the GHI but was instead discharged with a reference to "mental incapacity" rather than insanity.

him he'll be d – d if he don't kill him." Cooper Lindsay of Columbus demonstrated what whites meant. Encountering Private James Gant on the street, Lindsay called him a "God damn black son of a bitch" for "not giving [Lindsay] more room for passing"; when Gant drew his bayonet, Lindsay shot him three times. Gant survived, but David Bracker was less fortunate. Serving with the 39th US Colored Infantry in North Carolina, Bracker was shot and killed by "a noted rebel." No one knew when an ordinary encounter might erupt into lethal violence (Figure 6.2).[13]

None of the insanity cases made explicit reference to the trials of occupation duty, but potential traces appear. Joseph

---

[13] Frederick Mosebach to A. R. Ninninger, July 24, 1866, Letters Sent, Columbus, Ga., Freedmen's Bureau subassistant commissioner, Bureau of Refugees, Freedmen, and Abandoned Lands, Records of Field Offices for the State of Georgia, 1865–1872, National Archives Microfilm Publication M1903, Genealogical Society of Utah; *Christian Recorder,* July 8, 1865; Berlin et al., *Freedom,* ser. II, 756–757. For a version of the Gant-Lindsay incident that lionizes Lindsay and reports that Gant was killed, see *Macon Weekly Telegraph,* Feb. 19, 1866. On the stresses of occupation duty, see Berlin et al., *Freedom,* ser. II, 733–737; Shaffer, *After the Glory,* 23–38; Reid, *Freedom for Themselves,* 284–286; Mark A. Bradley, *Bluecoats and Tar Heels: Soldiers and Civilians in Reconstruction North Carolina* (Lexington: University Press of Kentucky, 2009), 47–70; Glatthaar, *Forged in Battle,* 207–230; Gregory P. Downs, *After Appomattox: Military Occupation and the Ends of War* (Cambridge, MA: Harvard University Press, 2015), 191–192; Hannah Rosen, *Terror in the Heart of Freedom: Citizenship, Sexual Violence, and the Meaning of Race in the Postemancipation South* (Chapel Hill: University of North Carolina Press, 2009), 23–60.

Figure 6.2. Edmund Delaney was among thousands of black soldiers assigned to postwar occupation duty in the South; Delaney's regiment served in south Texas until 1867. From Service Record of Edmund Delaney, 117th US Colored Infantry, Record Group 94, National Archives

Shipley, whose mental illness is discussed later in this chapter, reportedly experienced a worsening of symptoms while serving in Texas. It is reasonable to implicate a malevolent populace in James Hall's "suicidal mania," and sensible to suspect immanent violence behind the actions of Benedick Antone. Antone stabbed his sergeant with a butcher knife and attacked his captain, resulting in the former's imprisonment and subsequent commitment to the Government Hospital for "homicidal mania." The traumas endured by African American occupation troops differed from, but were in their way equivalent to, those of warfare.[14]

Several instances illustrate the other pattern in the insanity cases. Henry Endicott's symptoms fit the contemporary definition of "mania." He was, according to a regimental surgeon, sometimes "a little rational, but for the most part is raving, and uncontrollable." His disorder was thus "manifest" and a threat to military effectiveness. Napoleon Bonaparte's condition sharpened the distinction between mania and other forms of mental illness. For a year following his enlistment in the 42nd Colored Infantry, Bonaparte showed "a sort of taciturn melancholy" but he was assigned regular duties. After talking to his long-absent father, however, Bonaparte "has been entirely insane," and he was soon sent to the Government Hospital with "acute mania."[15]

---

[14] Affidavit of Moses Shipley, May 6, 1895, Pension File of Joseph Shipley, 9th US Colored Infantry, RG 15, National Archives (hereafter cited as Shipley Pension File); Entry for James Hall, case no. 2366, GHI Register; Findings of General Court Martial, May 23, 1866, Service Record of Benedick Antone, 99th US Colored Infantry, Compiled Service Records; entry for Benedict Anthony [Benedick Antone], case no. 2513, GHI Register.

[15] Pease request, Service Record of Henry Endicott; Certificate of Insanity, Apr. 10, 1865, Service Record of Napoleon Bonaparte, 42nd US Colored Infantry, Compiled Service Records. On the "manifest" criterion, see Roberts Bartholow, *A Manual of Instructions for Enlisting and Discharging Soldiers* (Philadelphia: J. B. Lippincott, 1864), 237–238.

Table 6.1. *Diagnosed disorders of African American Civil War volunteers and a sample of white soldiers sent to the Government Hospital for the Insane*

Disorder	Number of black soldiers	Number of white soldiers
Mania	19	12
Dementia	8	8
Melancholia	0	7
Total soldiers	27	27

White soldiers provide a counterpoint. Despite a promotion to sergeant and a commendation for "gallant conduct" in several battles, David Sansenbaugh went to the Government Hospital suffering from "acute melancholia." Seymour Adams, after spending most of his enlistment in a regimental hospital, was transferred to the Government Hospital with a "mild type" of melancholia.[16]

These cases conformed to broader tendencies. Table 6.1 compares the 27 black soldiers committed by the army to

[16] Volunteer Descriptive List, Service Record of David Sansenbaugh, 23rd Kentucky Infantry, Compiled Service Records; Entry for David Sansenbaugh [given as George Sansebaugh], case no. 1823, GHI Register; W. W. Godding to Samuel Breck, Service Record of Seymour Adams, 1st Massachusetts Cavalry, Compiled Service Records; Entry for Seymour Adams, case no. 1976, GHI Register. Sansenbaugh was wounded in the neck at Chickamauga; Adams was released from the GHI and died of chronic diarrhea at age 19 (Massachusetts Registration of Deaths, 1841–1915, Genealogical Society of Utah).

the Government Hospital with an equal number of randomly chosen white inmates. The races were identical in the memory loss or confusion that were typically labeled dementia, but sharp differences emerge in the other mental illness categories. African Americans entered the asylum with more cases of mania than did whites, but with none of the depressive disorders that were typically identified as melancholia.[17]

It is conceivable that African Americans experienced mental illness differently, but two of the above cases suggest another explanation. Bonaparte suffered at first from melancholia, but he was left alone until he became "entirely insane." The white soldier Seymour Adams, on the other hand, was sent to the Government Hospital while his disorder was still "mild." These decisions accord with the pattern evident in Table 6.1: army officials were apparently ready to intervene for white soldiers with less disruptive psychological disorders, but were willing to wait until African Americans became intractable. In this way, and in the consequences of the postwar occupation of the South,

---

[17] Commitments and disorders from GHI Register. All black soldiers are included, except those with epilepsy and those from the regular army. White soldiers chosen at random from the same years (1864–1869) as the African Americans. On officials' belief that African Americans were especially susceptible to mania, see Summers, "Suitable Care"; John S. Hughes, "Labeling and Treating Black Mental Illness in Alabama, 1861–1910," *Journal of Southern History* 58 (1992), 435–460.

active-duty mental illness showed the imprint of the black military experience.

Physicians and Veterans Address Mental Illness

Two perspectives illuminate the struggles of black veterans with psychological disorders. The more familiar perspective is that of health professionals and their institutions. Insane asylums received African American veterans, but under different circumstances than during the war. The army sent 27 black soldiers directly to the Government Hospital; over the next quarter-century, when federal soldiers' homes were the chief conduit for inmates, only eight black veterans were committed. African American veterans were instead scattered in asylums across the nation. Inmates from the EI Colored Troops samples could be found in 17 states from Florida to Oregon.[18]

African Americans also came under the scrutiny of pension-examining boards. In the years before 1890 while pensions were restricted to war-induced conditions, physicians on these boards diagnosed some form of mental illness in approximately 1 percent of veterans in the EI

---

[18] Postwar commitments from GHI register. Sixty-seven members of the EI Colored Troops samples were known to have spent time in insane asylums; since they were pension applicants, their confinements tended to be in the late nineteenth and early twentieth centuries.

Colored Troops samples. This proportion equaled that of sample members who were confined in asylums, but was considerably less than the 6 percent of EI white sample members diagnosed with mental illness. Two factors offer clues to the discrepancy. African Americans with mental illnesses were more likely than whites to die before the late nineteenth century. Evidence is scarce, but mortality at the Government Hospital for the Insane hints at the difference. The asylum's death rate for African American veterans from 1866 to 1877 corresponds to 160 per 1,000 person-years, compared to 115 for white veterans. If fewer black veterans with psychological disorders were alive when pension-seeking became widespread, unbiased physicians would have reported fewer diagnoses.[19]

---

[19] Figures in this paragraph based on surgeon's certificates recorded in EI Colored Troops II (the earlier sample appears to have been transcribed differently) and EI White Troops. Indicators of mental illness include surgeons' diagnoses of insanity, depression, hysteria, and the like, but as noted above, we have excluded disorders stemming from epilepsy or sunstroke. Since we are analyzing pension applicants, we must recognize that white veterans, having begun their rush to apply earlier, had more examinations and thus more chances to be found insane. A separate analysis controlling for timing and number of applications (not shown) largely replicates the racial disparity in mental illness rates. GHI mortality from Board of Visitors of the Government Hospital for the Insane, Annual Reports, House Ex. Docs., 39th–45th Cong. (rate ends in 1877 because reports after that year no longer distinguished between Civil War veterans and those of the regular army). For comparison, the death rate for

But physicians were hardly unbiased. Where army doctors had focused on mania in their diagnoses of African American soldiers, Pension Bureau-appointed physicians were preoccupied with black veterans' alleged memory problems. Physicians complained that Edward Jones gave an "incoherent history" of his symptoms. George Brandy's responses to queries were "very vague and unsatisfactory," and Frederick Goldsborough could not "remember much such as age and events of military service." Nearly half of black veterans in the EI samples who had evidence of mental illness were diagnosed with memory loss, compared to 20 percent of whites.[20]

This fixation on defective mentality undoubtedly led physicians to overlook other disorders, as it did with Henry Burton. Surgeons examined Burton in 1885 for his claim of rheumatism, reporting that he "seems to be a little feeble-minded." Within months, however, Burton was transferred from a federal soldiers' home to the

---

black males reported in the registration states in the 1890 census was 34.5 per 1,000. US Census Office, *Report on Vital and Social Statistics in the United States at the Eleventh Census* (Washington, DC: Government Printing Office, 1896), Pt. I, 30.

[20] Surgeon's Certificate, Mar. 1, 1899, record of Edward Jones, 41st US Colored Infantry, ID 9004111162, EI Colored Troops II; Surgeon's Certificate, Oct. 18, 1905, record of George Brandy, 27th US Colored Infantry, ID 9002711118, EI Colored Troops II; Surgeon's Certificate, Oct. 12, 1904, record of Frederick Goldsborough, 39th US Colored Infantry, ID 9003903156, EI Colored Troops II.

Government Hospital because he was "insane, violent at times." Burton was said to be "very antagonistic to democrats individually and collectively" and had "delusions about pension business." Nor was Burton's condition a sudden eruption: asylum officials concluded that his "chronic mania" had lasted four years. Pension physicians' attention to Burton's intellect accompanied inattention to more serious problems. Multiplied enough times, such cases would account for much of the apparent racial difference in diagnosed mental illness.[21]

Pension records offer an alternative to the perspective of nineteenth-century experts. When applicants reported for a medical examination, they were to be "accorded the privilege of stating their cases. While their statements alone can not be regarded as a proper basis for rate, most of them can say something of importance bearing on their cases." Given this opportunity, veterans occasionally described psychological problems as evidence for a pension.[22]

The EI samples include verbatim transcriptions of these statements, which should be interpreted with caveats.

[21] Surgeon's Certificate, Jan. 14, 1885, Pension File of Henry S. Burton [Birton], 102nd US Colored Infantry, RG 15, National Archives; Entry for Henry S. Burton, case no. 6451, GHI Register; Case File of Henry S. Burton, case no. 6451, St. Elizabeths Hospital, Case Files of Patients, Record Group 418, National Archives.

[22] US Pension Bureau, *Instructions to Examining Surgeons for Pensions* (Washington, DC: Government Printing Office, 1887), 5.

Self-assessments for earlier decades are scarce because detailed statements began only in the 1880s. The statements were coached by claim agents, who knew the approach that would best secure a pension recommendation; statements were also frequently paraphrased by the physician who served as secretary for the examination.

Yet these realities make it all the more remarkable that veterans said anything about their mental illnesses. Claim agents surely knew about the paradox of psychological disorders – if a veteran suffered from a mental illness that would warrant a pension, he would presumably be incapable of making a coherent statement. Physicians found a few applicants who were thus incapacitated, but other pension-seekers explicitly cited psychological symptoms in their interview. These statements are the closest available approximation to self-narratives of veterans' long-term mental conditions.

Our focus is on veterans' connection of the war to difficulties with their heads and minds. Sixty-six African Americans and 124 whites in the EI samples made such statements; two-thirds of the black veterans had been slaves, approximately equal to the ex-slave proportion among all survivors. With one exception to be discussed below, applicants had no access to the vocabulary of contemporary alienists. Instead, a veteran might feel "very nervous" or "queer in his head" or "confused." Most of this vocabulary crossed racial lines. It is difficult to distinguish between Robert Jackson, who described a "nervous shock" which "came on his head while in service and is there yet," and John Anderson, who "had a sort of nervous spell" in battle that "lasted three hours repeated often since" (Jackson was African American, Anderson white).[23]

Yet racial differences emerge in assertions about cause and effect. Approximately two-thirds of both races blamed the major risks of war – wounds, disease, or injuries – for their mental difficulties. An additional one in eight whites, however, cited confinement as a prisoner of war, compared to none of the black veterans. Some of the African Americans had been captured and imprisoned, but they were far fewer than white ex-prisoners; their shorter wartime service and the Confederacy's avowed no-black-prisoner policy kept them to a minimum. Yet explaining applicants' statements is not so simple. Half of whites in the EI samples who cited psychological damage from confinement pointed to the Andersonville Prison, though only one-quarter of white ex-prisoners had been kept there. The ordeal of Andersonville may have been unique, but it is also possible that survivors sensed the infamous prison's potential for

[23] Surgeon's Certificate, Mar. 5, 1891, record of Robert Jackson, 14th US Colored Infantry, ID 9001406164, EI Colored Troops I; Surgeon's Certificate, May 18, 1887, record of John P. Anderson, 59th Illinois Infantry, ID 2105904001, EI White Troops. The quotes here are for comparison of medical vocabulary only; Anderson's full statement shows that his "nervous spell" came at the Battle of Stones River (Dec. 1862–Jan. 1863), which predated the extensive recruitment of black troops.

assisting a pension application (see Chapter 7 for further discussion).[24]

An equally sharp difference appears in veterans' declared symptoms. Without waiting for physicians to pass judgment, one in five white veterans identified their mental problems as "insanity." William Dunn explained that "a shell bursted over and near his head while in the service from which he became insane." Francis Buxton's disorder was more recent: in 1892 Buxton cited a head wound sustained at the Battle of Franklin, reporting that he "became insane as a result two or 3 years ago." Now his "mental condition varies, at times it is bad."[25]

These statements appear unremarkable, except by comparison with African American veterans. None of the black applicants, regardless of previous diagnosis or asylum confinement, used the term insanity in their statements

[24] On the Confederacy's no-prisoner policy, see John David Smith, "Let Us All Be Grateful That We Have Colored Troops That Will Fight," in John David Smith, ed., *Black Soldiers in Blue: African American Troops in the Civil War Era* (Chapel Hill: University of North Carolina Press, 2005), 45–49. Several members of the EI Colored Troops samples had been held in Andersonville, but none claimed mental illness. The figures cited here refer to veterans in EI White Troops and EI Urban Troops, so that prisoners and nonprisoners could be compared; for findings from EI Andersonville, see Chapter 7.

[25] Surgeon's Certificate, Jan. 14, 1891, record of William Dunn, 12th Illinois Infantry, ID 2101207129, EI White Troops; Surgeon's Certificate, April 27, 1892, Pension File of Francis M. Buxton, 64 Ohio Infantry, RG 15, National Archives.

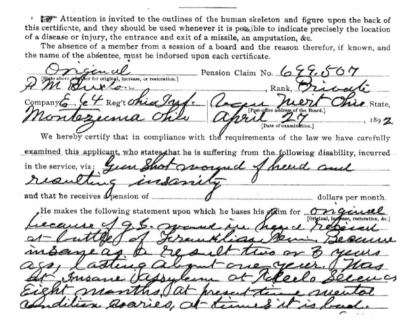

' ☞ Attention is invited to the outlines of the human skeleton and figure upon the back of this certificate, and they should be used whenever it is possible to indicate precisely the location of a disease or injury, the entrance and exit of a missile, an amputation, &c.

The absence of a member from a session of a board and the reason therefor, if known, and the name of the absentee, must be indorsed upon each certificate.

Pension Claim No.

[State above whether for original, increase, or restoration.]

, Rank,

Company____ Reg't____ [Post-office address of the Board.] ____ State,

____ , 189__

[Date of examination.]

We hereby certify that in compliance with the requirements of the law we have carefully examined this applicant, who states that he is suffering from the following disability, incurred in the service, viz:

and that he receives a pension of ____ dollars per month.

He makes the following statement upon which he bases his claim for ____

[Original, increase, restoration, &c.]

Figure 6.3. Claimant's statement recorded on the Surgeon's certificate for the pension examination of Francis Buxton. Unlike African Americans, a number of white veterans acknowledged "insanity" in their statements. Record Group 15, National Archives

(Figure 6.3). We lack additional testimony to establish the full meaning of this distinction, but we can revisit a similar disparity in the 1890 census. As we noted above, only 73 of the nearly 54,000 black veterans were reported as insane, half the rate found among whites. The pension statements demonstrate that African American veterans were willing to report symptoms associated with insanity, but they had little apparent willingness, either during a pension examination or a census-taker's visit, to accept the term. Black ex-soldiers may have understood, better than did whites, the potency of labels.[26]

"The Blacks Rarely Commit Suicide"

If noticeable racial differences appear in presentation and diagnosis of mental illness, there was a wider gap in reported suicides. Contemporary observers expressed opinions on suicide similar to those they had given about African American mental illness, with a similar inattention to veterans. Most commentators agreed with the historian who wrote that "the blacks rarely commit suicide" because "no cause of anxiety presses long enough upon the mind of the individual negro to foster a desire to put an end to life, this being another form of his inability to retain any one thought long enough to influence his conduct." A dissenting view pointed to the results of emancipation: "The equal rights mania has produced its effect. We have observed a number of cases of negro suicide recently." Apart from newspaper reports of

[26] US Census Office, *Report on the Insane, Feeble-Minded, Deaf and Dumb, and Blind in the United States at the Eleventh Census* (Washington, DC: Government Printing Office, 1895), 236; US Census Office, *Report on Population of the United States at the Eleventh Census* (Washington, DC: Government Printing Office, 1897), Pt. II, 803.

individual deaths, we have found no explicit commentary on black veterans' suicidal behavior.[27]

The EI samples offer a basis for comparing ex-soldiers' suicides. One former slave and 2 freeborn black men per 1,000 survivors took their own lives, compared to approximately 5 per 1,000 enlisted whites in the samples. Some of this difference may be due to missing deaths among black nonpensioners, but other sources suggest that it is broadly genuine. Both the EI samples and the *Medical and Surgical History* show lower suicide rates for black soldiers before pensions became an issue.[28]

---

[27] Philip A. Bruce, *The Plantation Negro as a Freeman* (New York: G. P. Putnam, 1889), 158; *New York Herald*, Feb. 24, 1869. For other discussions of black suicide's infrequency, see John T. Nagle, *Suicides in New York City during the Eleven Years Ending Dec. 31, 1880* (Cambridge, MA: Riverside, 1882), 8–9; US Census Office, *Report on Vital and Social Statistics of the United States at the Eleventh Census* (Washington, DC: Government Printing Office, 1896), 465; "Vitality of the Colored People," *New York Times,* Dec. 15, 1889. For another example of the opposite view, see *New York Sun*, Jan. 11, 1891.

[28] The EI figures were 1.1 per 1,000 for slaves and 2.2 for freeborn men. These probabilities are given per 1,000 so as to avoid confusing them with the usual rate of suicides per 100,000 of population; the figures here are cumulative probabilities, not comparable with yearly rates. Veterans included in the probabilities are those with known causes of death and, for African Americans, with an identified slave or free background. The wartime probabilities of suicide were 4.9 per 10,000 black enlisted men and 10.5 per 10,000 whites in the EI samples, and 4.9 and 11.6 from *MSH* (I: 712, 641).

If black veterans were less likely to die by suicide, then why? Part of an answer is rooted in a demographic reality. In any given year, African American veterans were more likely than whites to die from a cause other than suicide; the difference could approach 50 percent in the late nineteenth century. Some veterans who died, especially from rapidly progressing diseases such as pneumonia, might otherwise have killed themselves. The number of such cases is unknown, but they were more probable with African Americans' higher mortality.[29]

Modern historians have offered a different reason for black veterans' infrequent suicide. Their argument inverts the nineteenth-century presumption about race and self-destruction. Where white contemporaries saw African Americans' avoidance of suicide as a character defect, historians view it as a sign of superior resilience. Among civilians the resilience would have come from mutual

---

[29] Mortality estimates from EI White Troops, EI Urban, EI Colored Troops I and II. The near 50 percent figure is based on "hazard ratios," that is, the probability of dying in a given interval for black veterans compared to whites. The ratio of 1.48 for 1890–1894, for example, means that African Americans were 48 percent more likely to die in that period. Ratios late in the century were as follows:

1880–84	1.33
1885–89	1.38
1890–94	1.48
1895–99	1.28

support within a cohesive community; veterans enjoyed the extra benefit of wartime camaraderie and the satisfaction of having fought for freedom.[30]

This proposition is plausible but not readily testable. On the one hand, evidence exists for African Americans' consensus on suicide. When John Jackson shot himself in 1884, "the society and church of which Jackson was a member refused to turn out, as bodies." Jackson's death "greatly excited our colored population, and his act has been a topic of general discussion among them since. The colored people have but little sympathy for self-murderers."[31]

But the historians' argument also implies that suicide was rarer among black veterans than for civilians, an implication that is more difficult to assess. The annual number of African Americans who took their own lives was so small, especially if divided into veterans and civilians, that it would produce erratic rates. A reasonably satisfactory comparison

---

[30] Glatthaar, *Forged in Battle,* 237–238; David Silkenat, *Moments of Despair: Suicide, Divorce, and Debt in Civil War Era North Carolina* (Chapel Hill: University of North Carolina Press, 2011), 61–62. See also Dora L. Costa and Matthew E. Kahn, "Forging a New Identity: The Costs and Benefits of Diversity in Civil War Combat Units for Black Slaves and Freemen," *Journal of Economic History* 66 (2006), 936–962.

[31] *Palatka* [Fla.] *News,* Aug. 20, 1884. Whether Jackson was a veteran is unclear: an earlier report (*Palatka News*, Aug. 19, 1884) describes Jackson's background and makes no mention of military service, and it is impossible to determine whether he was one of the many John Jacksons in the Union army.

can be made, however, by combining person-years and suicides in the EI Colored Troops samples for 10 years centering
on 1890. The resulting rate can be compared to the 1890 census, the first enumeration to analyze suicide by race and age.
The EI calculation produces a suicide rate of 10 per 100,000
person-years; the 1890 census rate for African American
males was 6.2. Comparing rates with different derivations
can only be a rough approximation, but it nonetheless casts
doubt on the assumption that African Americans' military
experience conferred an extra immunity from suicide.[32]

Attributed suicide motives point in the same direction.
The small number of black suicides is further reduced by
sporadic news coverage, but accounts of 12 African American
veterans' suicides can be gleaned from newspaper reports.
Half of these deaths were blamed on ill health. Reporters
seldom described the decedents' malady or mentioned their
service. David Trail, who returned to his native Indiana
from the 14th Colored Infantry, had unspecified "low spir-
its induced by disease" when he shot himself in 1869. Allen
Green, who was wounded in the Petersburg campaign, was

[32] Veterans from the EI Colored Troops I and II samples reflected in
these calculations are those with known death dates and causes of
death; since the suicide tabulation covers 10 years and the census
rate 1 year, the EI rate is calculated on the basis of person-years
to standardize incidence and time. The census suicide rate is for all
black males (the rate was slightly higher, 6.8 per 100,000, for black
men from ages 15 to 45, with no suicides at older ages), in Census
Office, *Report on Vital and Social Statistics*, 463, 465. Census rates
are calculated from reports filed in five major cities plus New Jersey.

simply described as "demented from disease" when he lay down in front of a train.[33]

A perusal of nonveterans' suicides finds fewer health problems and a wider variety of such motivations as domestic conflict and grief over a loved one's death. These findings are at best suggestive, but since health problems were more common in veterans than civilians, the newspaper reports accord with the rates described above in hinting at a higher rather than lower incidence of suicide among black veterans.[34]

Nor did service with the US Colored Troops immunize white officers from later troubles. Historian Joseph Glatthaar has called attention to former USCT officers whose lives descended into substance abuse, divorce, or suicide. The EI samples bear out the suicide finding, so long as the point of comparison is African American veterans. The cumulative suicide probability in the EI samples, given above as 1–2 suicides per 1,000 black veterans, was more than 9 per 1,000 among former US Colored Troops officers. The samples also afford instances of domestic discord and drug and alcohol abuse. James Bacon, a former lieutenant in the 36th Colored Infantry, was "for a number of years addicted to both morphine and whiskey habits." James Adams was "a heavy drinker and while drinking is very

[33] *Indianapolis Journal,* Apr. 12, 1869; *Baltimore Sun*, Dec. 27, 1906.
[34] For examples of black nonveterans' suicides attributed to domestic disputes and grief, see *Omaha Bee,* July 11, 1890, Aug. 3, 1886.

abusive and quarrelsome." Adams frequently summoned his son and other relatives "to get him out of trouble and saloon brawls," and he and his wife separated in 1905.[35]

Yet it would be premature to conclude that the US Colored Troops attracted men with dysfunctional personalities or that they were tainted by leading black soldiers. Based on the EI samples, white officers' marriages were somewhat less likely than those of African American troops to end in separation or divorce. For every alcoholic or drug-addicted USCT officer, one can find a Theodore Stratton, a former captain in a white regiment who "went on periodical drinking sprees that could last for weeks" and then abandoned his family. USCT officers' propensity for suicide, so much higher than among black soldiers, was comparable to that of white regiments' officers. Nor were former USCT officers significantly more likely than other officers to be diagnosed with a mental illness in a pension examination. The only genuine distinction, that of postwar suicides, apparently lay in African Americans' disinclination to die by suicide rather than in officers' idiosyncrasies.[36]

---

[35] Surgeon's Certificate, June 6, 1891, record of James N. Bacon, 36th US Colored Infantry, ID 9003609106, EI Colored Troops II; Affidavit of Aug. 1, 1913, excerpted in record of James M. Adams, 25th US Colored Infantry, ID 9002511103, EI Colored Troops II. Suicide probability for officers included in EI Colored Troops I and II (survivors of the war, cause of death known) was 9.6 per 1,000.

[36] Affidavit of Aug. 25, 1915, excerpted in record of Theodore F. Stratton, 69th Pennsylvania Infantry, ID 1406911060, EI White Troops. Ten percent of officers' marriages in EI Colored Troops I and II

Patterns and Variations

Discussions of collective tendencies in mental illness and suicide tend to neglect the nature of their development and their erratic reflection in the evidence. Joseph Shipley personified these realities. On the one hand, the evidence is clear on the outlines of Shipley's life. He and his siblings grew up near Baltimore as slaves of a wealthy planter, who "kept [Joseph] and the other brothers with him in confinement to prevent their running away and joining the army." Three of the brothers nonetheless managed to enlist in the 9th Colored Infantry in November 1863, and Joseph was soon promoted to sergeant. William Shipley was killed in action near Petersburg in 1864 and Joseph and Moses served out their enlistments, returning to Maryland at the end of 1866. Joseph began to behave strangely, then violently, assaulting family members and setting fire to a barn. He was arrested and committed to a series of insane asylums where he spent the remainder of his 89 years.[37]

If we probe the nature of Shipley's disorder, however, biographical facts give way to a tangle of assertions. Moses

---

ended in separation or divorce, compared to 12 percent of enlisted men's marriages. The statistic p, the probability that a difference is due to chance rather than to a genuine characteristic of the whole Union army, is .549 for suicides among USCT officers versus officers in white regiments, and .565 (controlling for age) for mental illness diagnoses; a p of .05 or less is typically required for an assumption of significance.

[37] Affidavit of Mary Robinson, Jan. 15, 1898, Shipley Pension File.

Shipley declared that Joseph showed strange behavior in the trenches at Petersburg and worsening symptoms during occupation duty in Texas; several members of the Shipleys' company insisted that he displayed no odd behavior at all. One neighbor testified that Joseph was "clearly suffering from mental trouble" just after his return, and "any one could have told in a few minutes that he was not of right mind"; another acquaintance recalled seeing Shipley at about the same time, and "he appeared to be all right. I then talked with him and noticed nothing wrong." Joseph Shipley (or someone on his behalf) informed a census-taker in 1890 that he was "driven crazy by the noise of war." Physicians examining Shipley for a pension concluded instead that his "active dementia" came from "an inherited cerebral defect" (Figure 6.4).[38]

A record as extensive as Joseph Shipley's is almost too rich, threatening to confound rather than enlighten. It is at this point that broader tendencies are their most helpful. Moses Shipley blamed the onset of his brother's

[38] Affidavits of Moses Shipley, May 6, 1895, Thomas Knock, Sept. 22, 1898, Horace Price, Oct. 3, 1898, Thomas H. Day, Mar. 22, 1898, James Harris, Feb. 12, 1898, William Hampton, Feb. 1, 1898, Sandy Moore, Feb. 8, 1898, Samuel Jones, Feb. 11, 1898, John Fowler, Feb. 10, 1898, Edward Waters, Feb. 22, 1898, Mat Roxbury, Feb. 10, 1898, John Maddox, Feb. 11, 1898, Hamilton Dashiell, Feb. 11, 1898, Ellen Reynolds, Aug. 3, 1893, Shipley Pension File; Surgeon's Certificate, June 19, 1893, Shipley Pension File; US Census of Union Veterans and Widows of the Civil War, 1890, National Archives Microfilm Publication M123, Genealogical Society of Utah.

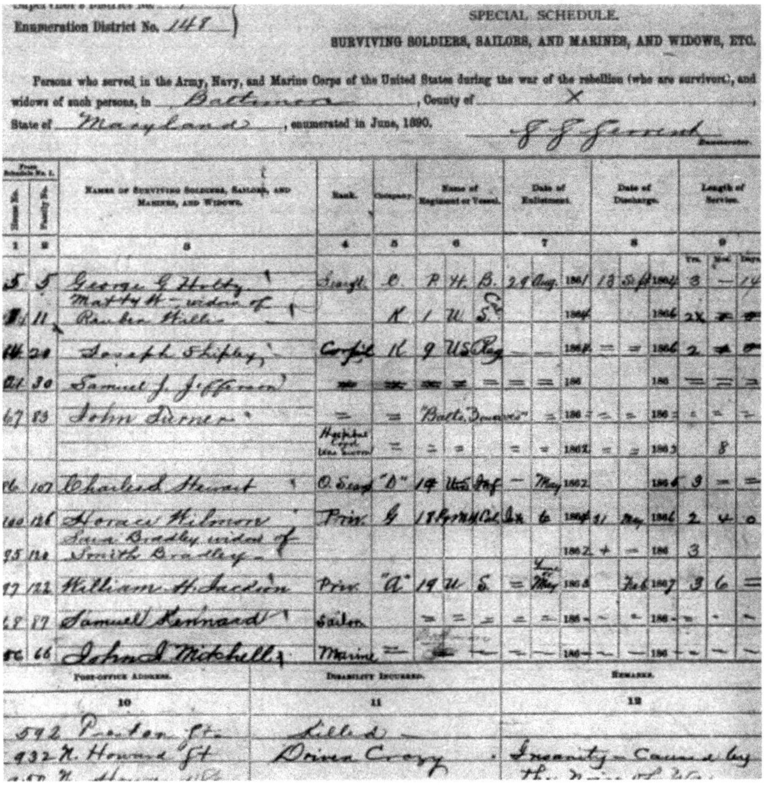
Enumeration District No. 148

SPECIAL SCHEDULE.

SURVIVING SOLDIERS, SAILORS, AND MARINES, AND WIDOWS, ETC.

Persons who served in the Army, Navy, and Marine Corps of the United States during the war of the rebellion (who are survivors), and widows of such persons, in Baltimore, County of X, State of Maryland, enumerated in June, 1890.

Names of Surviving Soldiers, Sailors, and Marines, and Widows. | Rank. | Company. | Name of Regiment or Vessel. | Date of Enlistment. | Date of Discharge. | Length of Service.

George G Holtz

Mattie H – widow of Reuben Hill

Joseph Shipley

Samuel J. Jefferson

John Turner

Charles Hewart

Horace Wilmore

Sara Bradley widow of Smith Bradley

William H. Jackson

Samuel Kennard

John A. Mitchell

Post-Office Address. | Disability Incurred. | Remarks.

592 Preston St. | Killed

432 N. Howard St | Driven Crazy | Insanity – Caused by

Figure 6.4. Page from the federal veterans' census of 1890, Joseph Shipley of the 9th US Colored Infantry listed as the fourth entry and remarks below. Shipley, an inmate of the Bayview Asylum in Baltimore, was reportedly "driven crazy" by "the noise of war." US Census of Union Veterans and Widows of the Civil War, National Archives Microfilm Publication M123 symptoms on "the roaring of the cannon" at Petersburg, which made Joseph strike "the front and back of his head with his hand frequently." Though examining physicians later dismissed this origin, veterans of both races took it seriously. John Lyons claimed that he had been "shocked by a cannon" that damaged his hearing, and "about every two months I go crazy." Charles Rice declared that his "whole trouble came from the sound of discharge of cannon at Richmond," and that he had been "troubled ever since by pain all over head."[39]

Moses Shipley's attribution is further substantiated by Joseph's postwar behavior. Witnesses recalled that before becoming violent, Joseph "imagined himself in the army." He "would walk up and down the street shooting with [a] stick," shouting "Grant says blow em up." Other ex-soldiers similarly relived their war. Michael Hogan, a white veteran from New York, kept "fighting over again the battles of his country." With a broom "or some similar weapon, he would go through the manual of arms." Wait Hastings, who had been held in the notorious Libby prison in Richmond, "would

---

[39] Affidavit of Moses Shipley, May 6, 1895, Shipley Pension File; Surgeon's Certificate, Nov. 5, 1890, record of John H. Lyons, 79th US Colored Infantry, ID 9007908162, EI Colored Troops I; Surgeon's Certificate, Nov. 5, 1890, record of Charles F. Rice, 69th New York Infantry, ID 1306909101, EI White Troops. On the noise of combat in soldiers' experience, see Earl J. Hess, *The Union Soldier in Battle: Enduring the Ordeal of Combat* (Lawrence: University Press of Kansas, 1997).

hide when a stranger came around for fear of being recaptured. He would also say that bloodhounds and the rebels were after him."[40]

The Pension Bureau rejected Moses Shipley's request, acting as Joseph's guardian, to increase Joseph's payment due to the wartime origin of his behavior. The Bureau's reading of the evidence was constricted: officials made no apparent effort to reconcile some witnesses' claim that Joseph had had no breaks in his service with a comrade's recollection that Shipley had been relieved of duty during a hospital stay. A broader interpretation places Joseph Shipley with other veterans who lived in the extended grip of the Civil War.[41]

Shipley illustrates another of black veterans' circumstances. In the 1910 federal census, the first extant identification of institutions and veterans, Shipley was the only African American veteran in the Maryland Hospital for the Insane. Only two white veterans were identified there as well, raising doubts about a racial difference among asylum-confined veterans.[42]

---

[40] Affidavits of Edward Shipley, Apr. 21, 1903, Henry Holland, Moses Steward, Moses Joyce, Apr. 20, 1903, Shipley Pension File; Surgeon's Certificate, Nov. 4, 1890, Pension File of Michael J. Hogan, 100th New York Infantry, RG 15, National Archives; Affidavit of Sept. 23, 1903, excerpted in record of Wait Hastings, 21st Michigan Infantry, ID 2402111042, EI White Troops.

[41] Affidavit of Samuel Jones, Feb. 11, 1898, Shipley Pension File.

[42] The 1910 federal census was notoriously deficient in its count of Civil War veterans, producing a result that was disowned by the Census Bureau; see Larry M. Logue, "Confederate Survivors and

The difference emerges, however, in asylums elsewhere. The aforementioned scattering of African American asylum inmates in the EI samples hints at their isolation. White inmates were also dispersed across numerous asylums, but they were more likely to be confined with fellow veterans. Binghamton State Hospital housed 23 white veterans and one black ex-soldier in 1910. The Pennsylvania Hospital for the Insane held nine whites and one African American veteran. The Kansas State Insane Asylum had seven white veterans and two African Americans. Central State Hospital, designated as the African American asylum for Virginia, housed only one black veteran in 1910. We can only speculate about the psychological effect of black veterans' sequestration from former comrades. Considering veterans' enthusiasm for groups such as the Grand Army of the Republic, however, the absence of fraternal opportunities was undoubtedly an additional hardship for black asylum inmates.[43]

---

the 'Civil War Question' in the 1910 Census," *Historical Methods* 34 (2001), 89–93. Enumerators of insane asylums appeared to take an all-or-none approach to the veteran question; census-takers at institutions reported here appear to have diligently applied the question. All institutional figures in this paragraph from US Census, 1910, National Archives Microfilm Publication T624, Genealogical Society of Utah.

[43] On veterans' enthusiasm for fraternal organizations, see Stuart McConnell, *Glorious Contentment: The Grand Army of the Republic, 1865–1900* (Chapel Hill: University of North Carolina Press, 1992); Gannon, *Won Cause.*

Conclusion

The incidence of black veterans' psychological disorders may be clouded by race-based differences in presentation, diagnosis, and circumstances, but these distinctions are meaningful. Physicians' preoccupation with African Americans' supposed memory problems helps to explain the apparent infrequency of other conditions. Black veterans' isolation in insane asylums helps to account for their reluctance to specify insanity on pension applications.

Veterans also had some control over how to end their lives, and black ex-soldiers chose suicide less often than did whites. Other racial distinctions may be plausibly explained by African Americans' treatment at the hands of a prejudiced medical profession. Our best estimate is that the trauma of the Civil War was no respecter of black or white skin, or slave or free birth.

7

Heavy Laden

T he present casts a long shadow. Seeking lessons from history is a popular pastime that exasperates historians. They understand that culling guidance from the past can mistake coincidence for continuity and misrepresent history. Akin to the indictments discussed in the Introduction, suspicion of specious analogies complicates interpretation of our findings.

But complication need not spell doom. Skepticism notwithstanding, connections to the present have never been entirely off limits for historians. Recent invocations of "agency" offer a case in point. Arising in studies of slavery, the salience of individual action has become a "master narrative." When slaves broke a tool or attempted an abortion or ran away or murdered an owner, they asserted human worth and subverted slavery. Exponents of this view make few claims about relevance to the present, but the implications are inescapable. Subjugated people have rejected victimhood in our own time, in a struggle that is as meaningful as the eventual achievement. Examining brutalized people in the past, scholars have found behavior hinting at a corresponding struggle. There is little need to spell it out: the instantly recognizable impulsion for human dignity is a corrective to portrayals of slaves as mere victims.[1]

This concept's reach may have exceeded its grasp. The crushing weight of slavery imposed a host of motivations for behavior; with testimony scarce, privileging deliberate resistance over other motives calls for a leap of faith. Agency is nonetheless widely influential and has appeared in studies of Civil War veterans. We will allude to the concept later in this chapter.[2]

Implied connections between past and present have their antithesis. In the Introduction we described current

[1] Walter Johnson, "Agency: A Ghost Story," in Richard Follett, Eric Foner, and Walter Johnson, eds., *Slavery's Ghosts: The Problem of Freedom in the Age of Emancipation* (Baltimore: Johns Hopkins University Press, 2011), 8–30 (quote on p. 8).

[2] The most pointed criticisms of the use of agency are Johnson, "Agency," and Walter Johnson, "On Agency," *Journal of Social History* 37 (2003), 113–124. Instances of the concept's appearance in reference to Civil War veterans include Wayne Wei-Siang Hsieh, "'Go to Your Gawd Like a Soldier': Transnational Reflections on Veteranhood," *Journal of the Civil War Era* 5 (2015), 558–559; Donald R. Shaffer, *After the Glory: The Struggles of Black Civil War Veterans* (Lawrence: University Press of Kansas, 2004), 131–132.

assumptions about posttraumatic stress disorder, especially the contention that its incidence is unprecedented. With our findings as a backdrop, this explicit denial of a link with the past invites the first of our closing questions. Should we conclude that Union veterans experienced PTSD?

Timeless or Transient?

Posing the question of PTSD revisits a debate on continuity of knowledge and experience. Advocates of continuity maintain that PTSD is merely the latest label for an age-old condition. Symptoms associated with PTSD can be found in soldiers from antiquity to modern times, including the American Civil War. The condition is an integral form of warfare's collateral damage.[3]

Opponents counter that PTSD is a diagnosis intentionally tailored to contemporary knowledge about anxiety

[3] Jonathan Shay, *Achilles in Vietnam: Traumatic Stress and the Undoing of Character* (New York: Atheneum, 1993); Matthew J. Friedman, "Veterans' Mental Health in the Wake of War," *New England Journal of Medicine* 352 (2005), 1287–1290; Eric T. Dean Jr., *Shook over Hell: Post-Traumatic Stress, Vietnam, and the Civil War* (Cambridge, MA: Harvard University Press, 1997); Richard A. Kulka et al., *Trauma and the Vietnam War Generation: Report of Findings from the National Vietnam Veterans Readjustment Study* (New York: Brunner Mazel, 1990), 284–285; Michael Sturges, "Post-Traumatic Stress Disorder in the Civil War: Connecticut Casualties and a Look into the Mind," in Matthew Warshauer, ed., *Inside Connecticut and the Civil War: Essays on One State's Struggles* (Middletown, CT: Wesleyan University Press, 2013), 159–180.

disorders. Devising a retrospective diagnosis based on coincident symptoms ignores fundamental changes in interpretation of mental illness. The adoption of PTSD formulated a new logic for understanding anxiety disorders, meant to reassure veterans and others that distressing symptoms were a likely result of recollected traumatic events. The logic of the past located culpability for mental illness within the individual, presuming defects in heredity or character. Applying one era's causation to another's effects is anachronistic and illogical.[4]

Each side makes usable points; neither provides a full explanation. Arguments for the timelessness of PTSD flatten history into a one-dimensional landscape dominated by a single set of symptoms. In arguing that conditions such

---

[4] See esp. Allan Young, *The Harmony of Illusions: Inventing Post-Traumatic Stress Disorder* (Princeton, NJ: Princeton University Press, 1997), 3–6, 141–142; Ian Hacking, *Mad Travelers: Reflections on the Reality of Transient Mental Illnesses* (Charlottesville: University Press of Virginia, 1998); Ian Hacking, *Rewriting the Soul: Multiple Personality and the Sciences of Memory* (Princeton, NJ: Princeton University Press, 1995); Hsieh, "Go to Your Gawd Like a Soldier"; Patrick J. Bracken, "Post-Modernity and Post-Traumatic Stress Disorder," *Social Science and Medicine* 53 (2001), 733–743. On nineteenth-century theories of insanity, see Gerald N. Grob, *The Mad among Us: A History of the Care of America's Mentally Ill* (New York: Simon and Schuster, 1994), 55–78. Although Eric Dean's work is often cited by those arguing for PTSD's timelessness, he restricts his interpretations to Civil War veterans and emphasizes the contemporary belief in moral causation of mental illness; see Dean, *Shook over Hell*, 135–160.

as PTSD are products of their time, the opposing side offers more comfort to historians. And yet it begs a vital question: if anxiety disorders in the past were not PTSD, what were they? By itself, this model provides little guidance. The most it can venture is the candid assessment that before the late nineteenth century's paradigm shift on the nature of memory, there was "unhappiness, despair, and disturbing recollections, but no traumatic memory, as we know it today."[5]

Two corollaries offer frameworks for a deeper probe of past psychological disorders. One such framework is "transient mental illness," posited by Ian Hacking to denote maladies that arise in a population and rapidly recede. Hacking's example is the putative epidemic of "fugue" centered in France at the turn of the twentieth century. Reified by European alienists, fugue impelled a number of socially marginal men to take lengthy journeys in a state of temporary insanity. Hacking maintains that fugue filled an "ecological niche." Such niches open when social and cultural tensions induce behavior that captures medical experts' attention; the niche for fugue closed in the early twentieth century as the phenomenon virtually disappeared.[6]

---

[5] Young, *Harmony of Illusions*, 141.
[6] Hacking, *Mad Travelers*, 51–79. For similar findings without the proposed generalizability, see Carroll Smith-Rosenberg, "The Hysterical Woman: Sex Roles and Role Conflict in 19th-Century America," *Social Research* 39 (1972), 652–678; Francis Clarke, "So Lonesome I Could Die: Nostalgia and Debates over Emotional Control in the Civil War North," *Journal of Social History* 41 (2007), 253–282.

Another framework takes the opposite tack. Instead of disorders that vanished, we can consider current diagnoses such as tuberculosis that were understood differently in the past, or autism, which was not a diagnosis at all. These diseases resemble transient mental illnesses in inviting close reading of cause and effect and context. Neither framework fully fits the psychological disorders of Union veterans, but taken together they point in a useful direction.[7]

The analogy with tuberculosis affords a viable starting point. The disease's symptoms today match those of the mid-nineteenth century. Beyond them, the names – tuberculosis versus consumption – hint at distinctive assumptions about origins, sufferers, and treatment.[8]

Within Contemporary Doctrines

So it was with Union veterans. As in prior studies, members of the EI samples experienced symptoms suggestive of PTSD. We saw in Chapter 6 that Joseph Shipley and others felt, in the words of the American Psychiatric

---

[7] On different understandings of tuberculosis, see Sheila M. Rothman, *Living in the Shadow of Death: Tuberculosis and the Social Experience of Illness in American History* (New York: Basic Books, 1994), 13–25, 179–193. For an example of comparative assessment of autism, see Cornelia H. Dayton, "'The Oddest Man That I Ever Saw': Assessing Cognitive Disability on Eighteenth-Century Cape Cod," *Journal of Social History* 49 (2015), 77–99.

[8] Rothman, *Shadow of Death*, 13–25, 179–193.3.

Association's *Diagnostic and Statistical Manual*, "as if the traumatic event(s) were recurring." Veterans could be tormented more generally by "intrusive distressing memories." Recollections of Daniel Penman's imprisonment "affected his youthful mind so much that he never forgot them." Penman repeatedly "spoke of the terrible shock they felt when the northerners killed their own buddies in prison for stealing rations from one another." Veterans might experience "recurrent distressing dreams," from which Michael Parantan "[woke] up screaming." They could react to "cues that symbolize or resemble an aspect of the traumatic event." After the "terror and shock" of an exploding shell that killed a comrade, Albrecht Mohr suffered from sleeplessness and was "irritable on hearing noise." Veterans such as Frederick Kampe and Andrew Helmick displayed "exaggerated negative beliefs." Kampe insisted that "his relatives are trying to injure him and rob him of a pension," and Helmick was convinced that he was "pursued by robbers and thieves and persons intending to do him bodily harm." "Angry outbursts" expressing "physical aggression" were likewise common. Helmick threatened "to kill and destroy human life," and Elias Brockway attacked his mother with an axe.[9]

---

[9] Affidavit, Dec. 30, 1936, record of Daniel Penman, 7th New York Heavy Artillery, ID 1311130751, EI Andersonville (see the appendix for full citation of EI samples); Surgeon's Certificate, Feb. 10, 1892, record of Michael Parantan, 104th New York Infantry, ID 1310408056, EI White Troops; Surgeon's Certificate, Dec. 14, 1891,

As with tuberculosis, psychological symptoms may match across centuries, but their root causes were understood differently. Nineteenth-century authorities searched reflexively for heredity and signs of moral weakness to explain veterans' mental illnesses. Elias Brockway seemed to display both tendencies. Pension investigators found insanity among Brockway's relatives, and examining physicians blamed his dementia on alcoholism. Brockway

---

record of Albrecht Mohr, 12th New Jersey Infantry, ID 1201209149, EI White Troops; Surgeon's Certificate, Feb. 10, 1866, record of Frederick Kampe, 59th Illinois Infantry, EI White Troops; Statement Alleging Insanity, Aug. 18, 1897, Pension File of Andrew J. Helmick, 186th Ohio Infantry, RG 15, National Archives; excerpted affidavit, Sept. 30, 1890, record of Elias E. Brockway, 15th Michigan Infantry, ID 2301504112, EI White Troops; *Diagnostic and Statistical Manual* quotes from American Psychiatric Association, *Diagnostic and Statistical Manual of Mental Disorders*, 5th ed. (Arlington, VA: American Psychiatric Association, 2013), Sec. 309.81. Previous studies that have identified symptoms resembling PTSD among Civil War soldiers and veterans include Dean, *Shook over Hell*; James Marten, *Sing Not War: The Lives of Union and Confederate Veterans in Gilded Age America* (Chapel Hill: University of North Carolina Press, 2011), 87–91; Diane Miller Sommerville, "'A Burden Too Heavy to Bear': War Trauma, Suicide, and Confederate Soldiers," *Civil War History* 59 (2013), 453–491; Michael W. Schaefer, "'Really, Though, I'm Fine': Civil War Veterans and the Psychological Aftereffects of Killing," in Lawrence A. Kreiser and Randal Allred, eds., *The Civil War in Popular Culture: Memory and Meaning* (Lexington: University Press of Kentucky, 2014), 11–23; Sturges, "Post-Traumatic Stress Disorder."

had been "repeatedly in jail for drunkenness" and was "considered a terror to the children in his neighborhood."[10]

If innate origins were ruled out, service-connected traumas could be blamed for veterans' symptoms. Encouraged by current dogma and constrained by pension regulations, Union veterans and physicians tried to link mental illness to diseases and wounds. Sometimes veterans themselves furnished the connection. John Blair claimed that he had "incurred typhoid fever diarrhea and general debility resulting in insanity" in 1862. William Webb, a veteran of the 13th Colored Infantry, complained that "his head was wrong since he was hit on it in battle at Nashville." John Martin's head wound left him "extremely irritable depressed in mind."[11]

More often it was pension physicians who avouched the link. They concluded that Ansel Wass's "chronic and probably incurable insanity" came from a head wound. Calvin Terwilliger's dementia was "a sequel of an attack of mania and the mania due to failure to take sufficient nourishment

[10] Excerpted affidavit, Nov. 28, 1890, Surgeon's Certificate, Mar. 15, 1893, Elias Brockway record.

[11] Surgeon's Certificate, May 2, 1883, record of John T. Blair, 43rd Indiana Infantry, ID 2204304020, EI White Troops; Surgeon's Certificate, Jan. 8, 1890, record of William Webb, 13th US Colored Infantry, EI Colored Troops II; Surgeon's Certificate, May 26, 1890, record of John E. Martin, 20th Michigan Infantry, ID 2300202099, EI White Troops.

Figure 7.1. Photograph of Andersonville Prison by A. J. Riddle, August 1864. Civil War Treasures Collection, New-York Historical Society

and debilitating effects of chronic diarrhea." Most attributions of psychological disorders, by veterans and by surgeons, kept well within the contemporary doctrine of organic origins.[12]

"Broken Down by Prison Life"

But not all attributions. Physicians were capable of disregarding medical dogma, especially for survivors of the Andersonville prison camp (Figure 7.1). Confinement as a

---

[12] Surgeon's Certificate, June 23, 1881, record of Ansel D. Wass, 19th Massachusetts Infantry, ID 0301911101, EI White Troops; Surgeon's Certificate, Apr. 24, 1890, Pension File of Calvin Terwilliger, 21st Michigan Infantry, RG 15, National Archives.

prisoner of war is typically harrowing, but Andersonville came to be the icon of Civil War inhumanity. We have seen in Chapter 6 that pension applicants who had survived Andersonville were more likely than those held elsewhere to mention their captivity, and examining surgeons likewise treated its aftermath as extraordinary.[13]

Physicians frequently conceded that the usual protocols were inadequate for evaluating Andersonville survivors. Surgeons tried to apply the usual etiology to Daniel Penman's insanity. Finding nothing hereditary and nothing amiss in the physical assessment, they were left to conclude that the origin was "unknown although his friends claim it as due to long confinement at Andersonville Prison." When Milton Ellsworth revealed that he had spent 10 months in Andersonville, his examiners admitted that "as a prisoner at Andersonville for a long time, [Ellsworth] is probably more seriously affected than is indicated by objective symptoms." Another panel acknowledged that Michael Nellis "has a history of great suffering in prison at Andersonville . . . We think it probable that his nervous disease dates from this experience." When George Farrar returned from eight months in Andersonville, "his nervous system [was] completely broken

---

[13] On Andersonville's iconic status, see, e.g., William Marvel, *Andersonville: The Last Depot* (Chapel Hill: University of North Carolina Press, 1994), ix–xi; Benjamin G. Cloyd, *Haunted by Atrocity: Civil War Prisons in American Memory* (Baton Rouge: Louisiana State University Press, 2010), 31–55.

down by prison life." Physicians diagnosed Farrar's condition as "a form of emotional insanity." They might have dismissed his case as "hysteria," but they recommended a pension for nervous disease.[14]

These explanations point to a broader tendency. Andersonville survivors were more than twice as likely as nonprisoners to be diagnosed with a mental illness. "Moral injury" is a modern term for severe violations of soldiers' moral compass, but Union veterans and physicians apprehended something similar. They acted on the conviction that the extraordinary torments of Andersonville were enough to produce psychological disabilities.[15]

---

[14] Surgeon's Certificate, June 30, 1891, record of Daniel Penman; Surgeon's Certificate, Dec. 24, 1890, record of Milton Ellsworth, 19th Massachusetts Infantry, ID 0311117707, EI Andersonville; Surgeon's Certificate, Mar. 8, 1899, record of Michael Nellis, 27th New York Infantry, ID 1311116366, EI Andersonville; Affidavit, Aug. 1, 1886, Surgeon's Certificate, Nov. 23, 1898, record of George W. Farrar, 4th Massachusetts Cavalry, ID 0311117504, EI Andersonville.

[15] The mental illness comparison is based on the EI White Troops sample, since EI Andersonville is restricted to those who lived to 1900. Among pension applicants, 5.9 percent of nonprisoners were diagnosed at least once with a mental illness, 6.8 percent of prisoners confined elsewhere were so diagnosed, and 12.9 percent of Andersonville survivors received a mental illness diagnosis. See also Dora L. Costa and Matthew E. Kahn, "Surviving Andersonville: The Benefits of Social Networks in POW Camps," *American Economic Review* 97 (2007), 1467–1487. On moral injury, see Brett T. Litz et al., "Moral Injury and Moral Repair in War Veterans: A Preliminary Model and Intervention Strategy," *Clinical Psychological Review* 29 (2009), 695–706; Jonathan Shay, *Achilles in Vietnam:*

PTSD and Complexity

Andersonville cases indicate that physicians and veterans were not blind to the potency of traumatic recollections. Yet their significance should not be exaggerated: posttraumatic reactions were marginal to the heredity-morality-organic axis of mental illness. By most assumptions, the investigation should end here. Tantalizing anecdotes notwithstanding, PTSD belongs to our own time. Union veterans belonged to an era with its own terms and conditions, which should be respected rather than subordinated to the present.

Fair enough, but respect includes acknowledging contrary evidence. Isaac Stearns and Horace Porter, the advocates we discussed in Chapter 5, offered two extraordinary observations. At a time when the traumas of war were considered adjuncts to the real origins of insanity, Stearns and Porter elevated them to triggers of a new syndrome. Emending the received triumvirate of melancholia, mania, and dementia, the two physicians posited a psychological disorder unique to veterans.[16]

Combat Trauma and the Undoing of Character (New York: Scribner, 1994), esp. 3–19; Kent D. Drescher et al., "An Exploration of the Viability and Usefulness of the Construct of Moral Injury in War Veterans," *Traumatology* 17 (2011), 8–13.

[16] I. H. Stearns, "A New Name for an Old Veteran's Disease," *Medical Summary* 10 (1888), 49–50; Horace P. Porter, "The Common Nervous Trouble of Old Soldiers," *Leonard's Illustrated Medical Journal* 10 (1889), 22.

Stearns and Porter made a second pregnant observation. Stearns claimed that his discovery represented "so many soldiers of the late war"; Porter declared that his findings were "so very common that they have been almost entirely overlooked." Both men understood that mental illness was as much a matter of epidemiology as of medical diagnosis.[17]

Stearns's and Porter's pleas for recognition sparked no diagnostic revolution, but they bring us back to our earlier questions. They accord with the evidence of this study in marginalizing – but not precluding – conditions suggestive of PTSD. Though the two physicians viewed veterans' symptoms through the prism of neurological damage, their logic was not incompatible with traumatic recollections. The stressors they identified included "the Neurokinesis of battle" and "severe mental strain"; the symptoms they reported included "susceptibility to unfavorable impressions," sleeplessness, and "a loss of power to concentrate the thoughts."[18]

Nor is it inconceivable that veterans themselves suffered from an equivalent to PTSD. Since the disorder is predicated on cause plus results, a collation of familiar symptoms is by itself unpersuasive. And yet there were Union veterans whose plight was convincing. Harrison Horr, reportedly haunted by accidently killing his brother, and Daniel Penman, allegedly tormented by memories of Andersonville,

[17] Stearns, "New Name," 49; Porter, "Nervous Trouble," 22.
[18] Porter, "Nervous Trouble," 22; Stearns, "New Name," 49.

likely met the preconditions for PTSD. They had no psychiatric vocabulary to help them understand their distress, but neither do modern veterans who happen to be unaware of PTSD.[19]

The time has come to abandon the PTSD-not PTSD dichotomy. It is insupportable to infer PTSD from every instance of nightmares and irritability, but it is equally insupportable to reject the disorder based solely on psychiatric paradigms. This subject is not a zero-sum competition between the past and the present. Acknowledging causes and consequences of traumatic reexperiencing merely illuminates the complexity of Civil War veterans' plight. The amply demonstrated gulf between the conceptual worlds of postbellum medicine and the late twentieth century offers a compelling perspective on the adoption of PTSD; the gulf between postbellum medicine and the conceptual world of ordinary veterans offers a compelling perspective on their suffering. When Union veterans provided glimpses of traumatic events and recurring distress, they revealed an inner torment that accords with the intent if not the semantics of PTSD.[20]

---

[19] On lack of awareness of PTSD among veterans, see, e.g., Nina A. Sayer et al., "A Qualitative Study of Determinants of PTSD Treatment Initiation in Veterans," *Psychiatry* 72 (2009), 238–255.

[20] For a similar argument about Confederate veterans, see Jeffrey W. McClurken, *Take Care of the Living: Reconstructing Confederate Veteran Families in Virginia* (Charlottesville: University of Virginia Press, 2009), 132–133.

Invoking complexity carries an obligation to gauge its extent. As we have found throughout this study, ordinary veterans' experience was refracted through multiple paradigms. Former Union soldiers had an exceptional opportunity to exercise agency by initiating pension requests, but their narratives of disability were influenced by pension policy and interpreted according to medical doctrine.

Veterans' records bear the imprint of these priorities. We have seen in Chapter 6 that two-thirds of EI sample members who complained of mental illness blamed disease, wounds, or injuries. Examining physicians were even surer of these culprits: when they disclosed reasons for mental illness diagnoses, they named disease, wounds, or injuries in nine of 10 cases. These may be suspected as biased judgments, but other evidence concurs. Twenty-five percent of EI sample members diagnosed with mental illness had been discharged for disability, compared to 16 percent of other veterans; moreover, more than half of the physical causes blamed for veterans' psychological symptoms were confirmed with approved pensions. The presence of physical disabilities in the lives of veterans with psychological disorders is unmistakable.

We may use this evidence to frame responses to our earlier questions. Drawing on physicians' judgments and veterans' testimony, we have identified ex-soldiers who apparently suffered from psychological distress. Their dominant feature, allowing for the pension system's preoccupation with physical disabilities, was the bodily damage of war. A substantial majority of veterans with mental illness symptoms lived with diseases such as rheumatism and diarrhea, wounds such as head wounds and amputated limbs, or injuries such as concussions from exploding ordnance. Others in this diverse population suffered psychological distress from a variety of origins, including recurrent memories suggestive of PTSD.[21]

Signature Disorders

It is accepted practice to identify signature mental illnesses for major wars. Shell shock characterizes World War I, combat fatigue defines World War II and Korea, and PTSD and traumatic brain injury symbolize recent conflicts in the Middle East. The Civil War produced no such mental illness hallmark. We have seen that diagnoses proposed by Isaac Stearns and Horace Porter fell on deaf ears. "Irritable heart," sometimes cited as a Civil War signature, relegated anxiety symptoms to insignificance against organic causes and

---

[21] For a similar argument about an African American veteran, see John David Smith, *Black Judas: William Hannibal Thomas and the American Negro* (Athens: University of Georgia Press, 2000), 271. On amputation and suicide among Confederate veterans, see Brian Craig Miller, *Empty Sleeves: Amputation in the Civil War South* (Athens: University of Georgia Press, 2015), 116–117.

effects. As a psychological disorder rooted in the era's domestic ethos, nostalgia is an appropriate hallmark for soldiers but excludes veterans.[22]

[22] For a summary of signature disorders through the Vietnam War, see Dean, *Shook over Hell*, 26–45; see also Tracey Loughran, "Shell Shock, Trauma, and the First World War: The Making of a Diagnosis and Its Histories," *Journal of the History of Medicine and the Allied Sciences* 67 (2010), 94–119; Jay Winter, "Shell Shock," in Jay Winter, ed., *The Cambridge History of the First World War*, 3 vols. (New York: Cambridge University Press, 2014), III: 310–333; Jonathan R. T. Davidson et al., "Symptom and Comorbidity Patterns in World War II and Vietnam Veterans with Posttraumatic Stress Disorder," *Comprehensive Psychiatry* 31 (1990), 162–170; Patricia B. Sutker and Albert N. Allain Jr., "Assessment of PTSD and Other Mental Disorders in World War II and Korean Conflict POW Survivors and Combat Veterans," *Psychological Assessment* 8 (1996), 18–25. On traumatic brain injury, see, e.g., Susan Okie, "Traumatic Brain Injury in the War Zone," *New England Journal of Medicine* 352 (2005), 2043–2047; Sharon B. Shively and Daniel P. Perl, "Traumatic Brain Injury, Shell Shock, and Posttraumatic Stress Disorder in the Military – Past, Present, and Future," *Journal of Head Trauma and Rehabilitation* 27 (2012), 234–239. Jacob Da Costa devoted four pages of his seminal article on irritable heart to a lengthy list of physical symptoms (rapid pulse, chest pain, and the like), compared to a half-page of symptoms of nervous stress. J. M. Da Costa, "On Irritable Heart: A Clinical Study of a Form of Functional Cardiac Disorder and Its Consequences," *American Journal of Medical Sciences* 61 (1871), 17–52. For examples of references to irritable heart as the Civil War's signature mental illness, see Kenneth C. Hyams, F. Stephen Wignall, and Robert Roswell, "War Syndromes and Their Evaluation: From the US Civil War to the Persian Gulf War," *Annals of Internal Medicine* 125 (1996), 398–405; Mark A. McCormick-Goodhart, "Leaving No Veteran Behind:

Uncertainty about the Civil War era might be blamed on primitive medical knowledge, but it also accords with the disparate causes of psychological distress among Union veterans. No single descriptor can encompass Calvin Terwilliger's path from disease to mania, John Martin's route from a head wound to depression, and Albrecht Mohr's passage from a shell explosion to irritability.

But Isaac Stearns and Horace Porter intimated another approach. Their references to the large number of war-connected psychological disorders reconnect with assertions cited in the Introduction. The urgency of PTSD and other invisible wounds in our own time is likewise a matter of incidence, but with an added dimension – the deadly unpredictability of modern wars allegedly produces more severe psychological casualties than did warfare in the past. This assumption implies that the real signature of a war's psychological toll is collective, in the accumulation of all mental illnesses among survivors. Competing allegations about

---

Policies and Perspectives on Combat Trauma, Veterans Courts, and the Rehabilitative Approach to Criminal Behavior," *Penn State Law Review* 125 (2012), 895–926; Sheena M. Eagan Chamberlin, "Emasculated by Trauma: A Social History of Post-Traumatic Stress Disorder, Stigma, and Masculinity," *Journal of American Culture* 35 (2012), 358–365. On nostalgia, see esp. Frances Clarke, "So Lonesome I Could Die: Nostalgia and Debates over Emotional Control in the Civil War North," *Journal of Social History* 41 (2007), 253–282.

warfare invite assessment: observations by Stearns and Porter about the prevalence of the Civil War's psychological aftereffects, versus the twenty-first-century conviction that contemporary conflicts' aggregate damage overshadows that of the past.

In Chapters 5 and 6 we estimated the incidence of Union veterans' mental illness diagnoses, but comparing severity calls for an added perspective. We have shown throughout this study that evidence on suicide broadens our grasp of the Civil War's psychological cost. It also deepens the complexity of mental illnesses. Veterans' suicides were a tangle of psychological disorders and deliberate agency, public knowledge and medical incomprehension, and changing circumstances over the life course.

Information on suicide nonetheless confers a measure of analytical clarity. Suicides were exempt from the skepticism that clouded the case of William Gould. In the attack on Wilmington, North Carolina, in early 1865, a shell exploded 50 feet from Gould's position. "The wind of the shell took off his cap," and later he "began to be troubled with dizziness which he has had ever since." Examining physicians, finding "no nervous phenomena," judged Gould's mental state to be "normal." Gould may actually have suffered from a mild traumatic brain injury, or he may actually have been unharmed; the reality cannot be settled without additional evidence. If Gould had died by suicide, speculation about normality would be moot. There was little agreement on what suicide was, but a broad consensus on what it was not – suicide was anything but normal.[23]

This icon of abnormality gains its special usefulness through aggregation and comparison. Causes other than the war could have led to Union veterans' suicides. If so, aggregating their deaths into rates and comparing with civilians should show little difference. Yet white veterans analyzed in Chapters 4 and 5 and African Americans discussed in Chapter 6 committed suicide at rates higher, sometimes much higher, than did civilian men.

On the other hand, these rates should pale to insignificance in comparison with suicides among recent veterans. We turn again to Massachusetts and its exceptional death records for the nineteenth century. Estimates by the Department of Veterans Affairs provide the number of veterans in 2014, and veterans' suicides are taken from the 18 states that make up the National Violent Death Registration System.[24]

---

[23] Surgeon's Certificate, Mar. 12, 1891, record of William Gould, 203rd Pennsylvania Infantry, ID 1420308028, EI White Troops. On popular ideas about suicide, see Chapter 3; on experts' disagreements, see Howard I. Kushner, *Self-Destruction in the Promised Land: A Psychocultural Biology of American Suicide* (New Brunswick, NJ: Rutgers University Press, 1989), 35–61.

[24] For sources of information on Massachusetts population and suicides, see Chapter 2. Data on veterans in 2014 from US Department of Veterans Affairs, Veteran Population Projection Model 2014, www .va.gov/vetdata/Veteran_Population.asp; data on veteran suicides from Centers for Disease Control and Prevention, National Violent

Table 7.1. *Suicide rates among veterans, Massachusetts quinquennial aggregate, 1870–1900, and National Violent Death Registration System states, 2014*

	Suicides per 100,000 veterans
Veterans in Massachusetts, 1870–1900*	45
White male veterans age 25+, NVDRS* states, 2014	37
African American male veterans age 25+, NVDRS* states, 2014	12

* *Note:* AK, CO, GA, KY, MA, MD, MI, NC, NJ, NM, OH, OK, OR, RI, SC, UT, VA, WI.

Table 7.1 shows the comparison of suicide rates. The rate for Massachusetts is a composite of those shown in Table 5.2 for federal and state census years. Rates for 2014 are divided by race to better compare with Massachusetts, where no suicides were recorded among black veterans in the included years. Union veterans' suicides considerably exceeded those for whites in 2014; the 2014 rate for African Americans was similar to the 10 per 100,000 estimated in Chapter 6. Since these rates have different derivations, they should be interpreted only for their broadest implication: veterans

Death Reporting System, www.cdc.gov/injury/wisqars/nvdrs.html. All states of the national reporting system are included in Table 7.1 because Massachusetts has become a modern outlier in the infrequency of its suicides; the state's rate for white male veterans older than 25 in 2014 was 14 per 100,000.

were laden with a distinctive burden in the late nineteenth century. The implications of this burden are the subject of our concluding reflections.[25]

---

[25] A recent citation of a suicide rate of 80 per 100,000 among veterans aged 18–29 (US Department of Veterans Affairs, Office of Suicide Prevention, "Suicide among Veterans and Other Americans, 2001–2014," Aug. 13, 2016, p. 32) has been carried in news reports; see Dave Philipps, "Suicide Rate among Veterans Has Risen Sharply since 2001," *New York Times,* July 7, 2016. The CDC reporting system and Veteran Population Model show a similar figure of 77 per 100,000 for 2014. These figures are questionable: grounds for suspicion begin with the unusually low suicide rate of approximately 20 for male veterans aged 30–39 in "Suicide among Veterans"; the CDC/Veteran Population Model rate is 35. Moreover, the CDC rates, and the standard death certificates on which they are based, make no distinction between current and former service members. Although "Suicide among Veterans," 5, implies an effort to establish this distinction, there is a suspiciously high correlation ($r = .72$) between suicides in the registration states and the number of active-duty personnel stationed there (personnel from Defense Manpower Data Center, Counts of Active Duty and Reserve Service Members and APF Civilians, 2017 [data for 2014]). The extent to which the extraordinary suicide finding for younger veterans is due to data limitations is thus unclear.

Conclusion: This Freedom from Insanity

This has been a study of multiple perspectives on troubled Union veterans. Friends, neighbors, and journalists were mainly sympathetic toward institutionalized veterans and those who died by suicide. Comrades frequently expressed support for veterans in distress, culminating in the advocacy of Isaac Stearns and Horace Porter.

Medical professionals' perspective exerted more influence, then and ever since. Led by asylum superintendents, experts dismissed war-connected psychological disorders. One administrator put the case succinctly: despite the "shock of many battles" and the hardships of camp life, long marches, and imprisonment, soldiers had "shown what true volunteers they are, and what patriots can do and suffer, and yet be strong." Their strength contributed to "this freedom from insanity."[1]

Examining physicians supplied an equally influential perspective. Some were veterans themselves, but all were expected to act as stewards of pension benefits. They could hardly accede to the freedom-from-insanity conceit, and their observations on mental illnesses have been essential to this study. Physicians' frequent failure to detect suicidal thoughts among EI sample members, however, signals the limitations of their perspective.

These actors touched the lives of ex-soldiers in distress, but we have tried throughout this study to recover the voices of veterans themselves. We conclude with a summation of what they evidently experienced.

Taken by themselves, Union veterans' psychological symptoms would encourage any advocate of the universal soldier. Pension statements and physicians' diagnoses reported depression, flashbacks, irritability, sleeplessness, and other indicators that seem to tie Union veterans' era to ours. But most causes of these symptoms were firmly situated in the nineteenth century. A few veterans could trace their distress to a traumatizing event or a blast-wave injury, but they were far outnumbered by psychological disorders originating otherwise. Mental illnesses arising from the pain

---

[1] Annual Report of the Managers of the State Lunatic Asylum, Documents of the Senate of New York, 87th sess. (1864), No. 35, vol. III, 41.

of an unhealed wound or the misery caused by diarrhea seem alien to twenty-first-century sensibilities, but such origins were often claimed by veterans and endorsed by physicians. The nature of these cases divorces them from later eras, and their wide variety precludes anointing any cause or symptom as a signature mental illness.[2]

Yet a postbellum hallmark need not be specified narrowly. Our findings on suicide suggest a defining feature of the Civil War's psychological harm. Few would disagree that suicide is the gravest fate of individuals in distress. Contemporaries routinely accepted the connection between insanity and suicide. Though examining physicians did a poor job of anticipating applicants' suicides, surgeons usually diagnosed a contributing nervous disorder when they detected suicidal intent. After a suicide occurred, acquaintances frequently came forward with testimony about decedents' insanity. These statements might be discounted as inventions for obtaining a pension, but they are corroborated by the wide gap between veterans' and civilians' suicide tendencies.

---

[2] For descriptions of the chronic miseries of wounds and disease, see Paul A. Cimbala, *Veterans North and South: The Transition from Soldier to Civilian after the American Civil War* (Santa Barbara, CA: Praeger, 2015), 87–91; Sarah Handley-Cousins, "'Wrestling at the Gates of Death': Joshua Lawrence Chamberlain and Nonvisible Disability in the Post–Civil War North," *Journal of the Civil War Era* 6 (2016), 220–242; Brian Craig Miller, "A Song for the Suffering: The Interminable Civil War," *South Central Review* 33 (2016), 53–68.

Conclusion

The Civil War's psychological cost is exemplified not by a single disorder but by the severity of veterans' mental illness in all its forms. A wide array of tangible and intangible damages afflicted the men we have encountered in this study. Their rate of suicides attests to the extraordinary affliction of some veterans and hints at a broader severity among others. This severity may have reflected the war's destructive force, or it may have been exacerbated by the lack of official acknowledgment. These possibilities are subjects for another study.

In response to the criticism that studies such as ours unduly emphasize the Civil War's dark side, we would argue that we are bringing veterans' untold sacrifices to light. Exploring some veterans' darkest miseries does not diminish the importance of others who unobtrusively lived their lives or achieved postwar distinction. They have had their chroniclers; our intent has been to underscore the diversity of veterans' life course, and to furnish benchmarks for a broader comprehension of their experience. This study is also far from a litany of victimization and fatal decisions. We can do no better than to commemorate troubled veterans and the men and women who came forward on their behalf. Having seen what war could do, they acted to make others understand.

Appendix: Sizing Up Sources

Studies that explore individuals' tendencies through quantitative evidence should describe its features and probe its weaknesses. *Heavy Laden* draws on several sources of such evidence. Some are manuscript and printed historical records, including vital statistics reports and death registers for Massachusetts; they are introduced and evaluated in Chapters 1 and 2. We have also used collections of historical evidence that has been digitized for researchers' use. Chapter 1 employs the Integrated Public Use Microdata Series, compiled by the Minnesota Population Center. The collection used here, known as IPUMS-USA, includes variables for randomly chosen individuals from each federal census.[1]

---

[1] Steven Ruggles et al., *Integrated Public Use Microdata Series: Version 6.0* (machine-readable database) (Minneapolis: University of Minnesota, 2015), www.ipums.org.

Appendix

The main digitized source for this study is a series of files produced for the Early Indicators of Later Work Levels, Disease, and Death project. The project, covering several decades of design, collection, and analysis, began at the University of Chicago's Center for Population Economics under the leadership of Robert W. Fogel. Researchers made an initial list of 331 randomly selected white infantry companies, then gathered military and pension records for each enlisted man in the companies (and some field officers, primarily those promoted from the ranks). The collection was eventually expanded with more soldiers – 169 companies of the US Colored Troops, plus samples of men who enlisted in the largest cities and survivors of Andersonville Prison – and an additional source, the US census.[2]

The resulting collection comprises five samples, referenced in this study as EI samples. The original sample, cited as EI White Troops, contains records for 39,341 enlisted men and officers. The US Colored Troops samples were collected in two phases and are cited as EI Colored Troops I and II;

---

[2] For overviews of the origins and course of the Early Indicators project, see Robert W. Fogel, "New Sources and New Techniques for the Study of Secular Trends in Nutritional Status, Health, Mortality, and the Process of Aging," *Historical Methods* 26 (1993), 5–43; Larry T. Wimmer, "Reflections on the Early Indicators Project: A Partial History," in Dora L. Costa, ed., *Health and Labor Force Participation over the Life Cycle* (Chicago: University of Chicago Press, 2003), 1–10; Dora L. Costa et al., "Union Army Veterans, All Grown Up," *Historical Methods* 50 (2017), 79–95. Information on latest additions to the project is available at www.uadata.org.

they contain records for 21,225 African American recruits and white officers. The urban sample, cited as EI Urban Troops, contains records for 12,671 recruits who enlisted in five major cities. The Andersonville sample, cited as EI Andersonville, has records for 1,003 survivors who survived to 1900.[3]

The EI samples offer extensive evidence on veterans' life course. Data collectors entered demographic and military information from soldiers' service records, and recorded census characteristics for sample members found in federal enumerations. When veterans applied for pensions, collectors entered particulars of the application and excerpted supporting testimony. Pension applicants also underwent medical examinations which assessed their claims for disability. The EI samples' summaries of examination findings are essential for analyzing diagnoses, and the verbatim

[3] Robert W. Fogel et al., *Aging of Veterans of the Union Army: Version M-5* (machine-readable database) (Chicago: Center for Population Economics, University of Chicago, 2000) (EI White Troops); Robert W. Fogel et al., *The Aging of US Colored Troops* (machine-readable database) (Chicago: Center for Population Economics, University of Chicago, 2004) (EI Colored Troops I); Dora L. Costa et al., *The Aging of US Colored Troops* (machine-readable database) (Chicago: Center for Population Economics, University of Chicago, 2015) (EI Colored Troops II); Robert W. Fogel et al., *The Impact of Urban Disparities on Aging and Mortality* (machine-readable database) (Chicago: Center for Population Economics, University of Chicago, 2015) (EI Urban Troops). Information on Andersonville sample at www.uadata.org/andersonville. EI research was funded by the National Institute on Aging.

transcriptions of applicants' statements present an invaluable reflection of ordinary veterans' state of mind.

The samples also require caveats. Information on veterans comes primarily from pension records, which are scarcer for the early years of restrictive pension requirements. This presents a particular problem in regard to African American veterans, whose pension-seeking lagged behind that of whites until the major liberalization of eligibility in 1890. Some veterans of both races did seek pensions in the initial postbellum years; we have used this information and other sources for insights into this crucial period. Afterward, as laws changed and more veterans applied for pensions, their characteristics and testimony afford a fuller portrait of middle-aged and older ex-soldiers. With suitable precautions, the EI samples provide an unparalleled account of Union veterans' experience.

Evidence of veterans' suicides in sources other than the EI samples also warrants caveats. Suspicions about the reporting of suicides are well known and are addressed in Chapter 2's investigation of death registration in Massachusetts. An equally important but much-neglected factor is the population at risk for suicide. Even when the number of suicides is reasonably trustworthy, a credible rate requires a credible count of veterans.[4]

---

[4] "At risk" is used here in the demographic sense that refers to everyone who is exposed to the event in question, rather than in the social welfare sense of those especially likely to experience it.

The federal census of 1890 was the first enumeration of Civil War veterans in Massachusetts, followed by the state censuses of 1895 and 1905 and a special tally in 1915. These counts present two types of problems. On the one hand, census directors repeatedly expressed reservations about the completeness of their enumerations. Since the federal Census Bureau was unable to compare the standard population schedules with special veterans' forms, "it must be understood that [counts of veterans] are approximate only." Since "no means of verification [were] available to the [Massachusetts labor statistics] Bureau," the state's 1895 and 1905 censuses "should be regarded as approximate rather than absolute." Bay State officials' suspicions about the 1915 census led them to enlist local tax assessors to help identify overlooked veterans.[5]

The second problem is the absence of any count of Massachusetts veterans in the quarter-century after the war. An adjacent state did enumerate its veterans in 1865: Rhode Island, 8 percent of whose veterans had served in

---

[5] US Census Office, *Report on Population of the United States at the Eleventh Census* (Washington, DC: Government Printing Office, 1897), Pt. II, clxxii; Massachusetts Bureau of Statistics of Labor, *Census of the Commonwealth of Massachusetts: 1895*, 7 vols. (Boston: Wright and Potter, 1896), I: 865; Massachusetts Bureau of Statistics of Labor, *Census of the Commonwealth of Massachusetts: 1905*, 4 vols. (Boston: Wright and Potter, 1909), I: cxviii; Massachusetts Bureau of Statistics, *A List of the Soldiers, Sailors, and Marines of the Civil War Surviving and Resident in Massachusetts* (Boston: Wright and Potter, 1916), 3–4.

Appendix

Table A.1. *Census identification of Union veterans*

Enumeration	Percentage identified as veterans	Number of veterans in sample
Rhode Island census, 1865	79	100
Federal census of veterans in Massachusetts, 1890	80	436
Massachusetts census of veterans, 1915	87	92

Massachusetts units, asked residents about their military service. This census can be used to estimate the larger neighbor's veterans, but along with the later enumerations it should also be evaluated for omissions.[6]

Evaluation is straightforward, beginning with known soldiers and seeking them in censuses. To frame the period covered by this study, we began with randomly chosen soldiers and looked for their listings in the Rhode Island census of 1865, the federal veterans' census of 1890, and the Massachusetts report of 1915. Table A.1 shows the percentage of veterans who were correctly identified in each year. One in five went unreported in the first two censuses; local officials' efforts improved the accuracy of the 1915 enumeration, but it nonetheless fell short of full coverage.[7]

[6] Rhode Island Secretary of State, *Report upon the Census of Rhode Island, 1865* (Providence, RI: Providence Press, 1867), 48.

[7] Rhode Island soldiers were chosen at random from *Annual Report of the Adjutant General of the State of Rhode Island* (Providence,

The suicide rates for Massachusetts discussed in Chapters 4, 5, and 7 compensate for these omissions. The total of army veterans in the Rhode Island census was first increased by the omission rate; the ratio of veterans to military-age men was then applied to the corresponding Massachusetts population to produce an estimate of 57,800 Bay State veterans in 1865. The Massachusetts veteran totals for 1890 and 1915 were similarly raised by their omission rates, and the veteran population in intervening years was estimated by interpolation. The approximate nature of these estimates precludes further distinctions by age groups.

RI: Providence Press, 1866). They were then sought in Rhode Island State Census, Microfilm F78, Rhode Island State Archives, http://search.ancestry.com/search/db.aspx?dbid=4721; the process was repeated until 100 soldiers were found in the census, with individuals classified as having their service reported or not. The starting point for Massachusetts veterans was all members of EI White Troops, EI Urban Troops, and EI Andersonville samples who appeared in the 1900 federal census as Massachusetts residents. With a few exceptions for recent in-migrants, these veterans should have been counted in the 1890 special census (US Census of Union Veterans and Widows of the Civil War, 1890, National Archives Microfilm Publication M123, Genealogical Society of Utah); their appearance or absence was noted. For 1915, the starting point was all members of the EI samples referenced above who appeared in Massachusetts in the 1920 federal census. Their appearance in or absence from Bureau of Statistics, *List of Soldiers*, was the basis of classification. Massachusetts censuses of 1895 and 1905 have not been made available in searchable form.

Appendix

Comparisons of suicide rates in this study use civilian men whose age range corresponds to that of veterans.[8]

[8] Since 98 percent of Massachusetts's adult male population was white in the late nineteenth century and no African American veteran suicides were recorded in the years studied, all analyses of Massachusetts suicides in Chapters 4, 5, and 7 refer to whites only. Chapter 6 takes up in detail the subject of African American suicide.

Bibliography

Primary Sources

Manuscripts

Countway Medical Library, Harvard University

Massachusetts Medico-Legal Society, Reports of Medical Examiners

Genealogical Society of Utah, Microfilm Collections, https://familysearch.org

Bureau of Refugees, Freedmen, and Abandoned Lands, Records of Field Offices for the State of Georgia, 1865–1872, National Archives Microfilm Publication M1903

Civil War and Later Pension Files, 1861–1917, National Archives Microfilm Publication T289

Massachusetts Registration of Deaths, 1841–1915

Massachusetts Registration of Marriages, 1841–1915

Massachusetts State Census, 1865

New York State Census, 1865

Registers of Veterans at National Home for Disabled Volunteer Soldiers, 1866–1938, National Archives Microfilm Publication T1749

Taunton State Hospital Patient Register, Microfilm 2108243

Bibliography

US Census of Union Veterans and Widows of the Civil War, 1890,
National Archives Microfilm Publication M123

US Census, 1860, National Archives Microfilm Publication M653

US Census, 1870, National Archives Microfilm Publication M593

US Census, 1880, National Archives Microfilm Publication T9

US Census, 1900, National Archives Microfilm Publications T623

US Census, 1910, National Archives Microfilm Publication T624

National Archives and Records Administration, Washington, DC

Civil War Compiled Service Records, Record Group 94

Civil War Pension Files, Record Group 15

St. Elizabeths Hospital, Case Files of Patients, Record Group 418

St. Elizabeths Hospital, Register of Patients, Record Group 418

Rhode Island State Archives, Providence

Rhode Island State Census, 1865, Microfilm F78

Government Reports

Bartholow, Roberts. *A Manual of Instructions for Enlisting and Discharging Soldiers*. Philadelphia: Lippincott, 1864.

Board of Managers of the National Home for Disabled Volunteer Soldiers. Annual Reports. House Miscellaneous Documents, Congressional Serial Set.

Board of State Commissioners of Public Charities of the State of Illinois. *Third Biennial Report*. Springfield, IL: State Journal, 1875.

—. *Seventh Biennial Report*. Springfield, IL: H. W. Rokker, 1883.

Board of Visitors of the Government Hospital for the Insane. Annual Reports. House Executive Documents, Congressional Serial Set.

[Boston] Discharged Soldiers' Home. *Third Annual Report*. Boston: George C. Rand, 1865.

DeBow, J. D. B. *Compendium of the Seventh Census*. Washington, DC: Beverly Tucker, 1854.

Defense Manpower Data Center. Counts of Active duty and Reserve Service Members and APF Civilians, www.dmdc.osd.mil/appj/dwp/dwp_reports.jsp.

Gould, Benjamin A. *Ages of US Volunteer Soldiery*. New York: US Sanitary Commission, 1866.

Harmon, Henry C. *A Manual of the Pension Laws*. Washington, DC: W. H. O. Morrison, 1867.

Hough, Franklin B. *Census of the State of New York for 1865*. Albany, NY: Charles Van Benthuysen and Sons, 1867.

Instructions for Taking the Census of the State of New York. Albany: Weed, Parsons, 1865.

Investigation of National Home for Disabled Volunteer Soldiers. House Report 2676, 48th Congress, 2nd session.

Journal of the Twenty-Fourth Annual Session of the National Encampment, Grand Army of the Republic. Detroit, MI: Richmond and Backus, 1890.

Managers of the State Lunatic Asylum. Annual Report. Documents of the Senate of New York, 87th session, Number 35.

Massachusetts Adjutant General. *Massachusetts Soldiers, Sailors, and Marines in the Civil War*. 7 vols. Norwood, MA: Norwood Press, 1931–1937.

—. *Annual Report of the Adjutant-General of the Commonwealth of Massachusetts*. Boston: Wright and Potter, 1866.

Massachusetts Board of State Charities. *Second Annual Report*. Boston: Wright and Potter, 1866.

Massachusetts Bureau of Statistics. *A List of the Soldiers, Sailors, and Marines of the Civil War Surviving and Resident in Massachusetts*. Boston: Wright and Potter, 1916.

Massachusetts Bureau of Statistics of Labor. *Census of Massachusetts: 1875*. 4 vols. Boston: Albert J. Wright, 1876.

—. *Census of Massachusetts: 1885*. 3 vols. Boston: Wright and Potter, 1887.

—. *Census of the Commonwealth of Massachusetts: 1895*. 7 vols. Boston: Wright and Potter, 1896.

—. *Census of the Commonwealth of Massachusetts, 1905*. 4 vols. Boston: Wright and Potter, 1909.

Massachusetts Secretary of the Commonwealth. *Abstract of the Census of Massachusetts, from the Eighth US Census*. Boston: Wright and Potter, 1863.

—. *Abstract of the Census of Massachusetts, 1865*. Boston: Wright and Potter, 1867.

Bibliography

—. *Reports to the Legislature of Massachusetts Relating to the Registry and Return of Births, Marriages, and Deaths in the Commonwealth.*

Medical and Surgical History of the War of the Rebellion. 6 vols. Washington, DC: Government Printing Office, 1870–1888.

Rhode Island Secretary of State. *Report upon the Census of Rhode Island, 1865.* Providence, RI: Providence Press, 1867.

Seaton, C. W. *Census of the State of New York for 1875.* Albany, NY: Weed, Parsons, 1877.

Superintendent of the St. Louis Insane Asylum. *Annual Report. Mayor's Message with Accompanying Documents to the Municipal Assembly of the City of Saint Louis.* St. Louis, IL: Nixon-Jones, 1887.

Trustees of the State Lunatic Hospital at Taunton. *Thirteenth Annual Report.* Boston: Wright and Potter, 1867.

—. *Eighteenth Annual Report of the Trustees of the State Lunatic Hospital at Taunton.* Boston: Wright and Potter, 1872.

Trustees of the State Lunatic Hospital at Worcester. *Thirty-Fourth Annual Report.* Boston: Wright and Potter, 1867.

US Census Office. *Manufactures of the United States in 1860.* Washington, DC: Government Printing Office, 1865.

—. *Statistics of the United States . . . in 1860.* Washington, DC: Government Printing Office, 1866.

—. *Ninth Census – Volume II: Vital Statistics of the United States.* Washington, DC: Government Printing Office, 1872.

—. *Statistics of the Population of the United States at the Tenth Census.* Washington, DC: Government Printing Office, 1883.

—. *Report on the Defective, Dependent, and Delinquent Classes . . . at the Tenth Census.* Washington, DC: Government Printing Office, 1888.

—. *Report on the Insane, Feeble-Minded, Deaf and Dumb, and Blind in the United States at the Eleventh Census.* Washington, DC: Government Printing Office, 1895.

—. *Report on Vital and Social Statistics in the United States at the Eleventh Census.* Washington, DC: Government Printing Office, 1896.

—. *Report on Population of the United States at the Eleventh Census.* Washington, DC: Government Printing Office, 1897.

—. *Twelfth Census of the United States: Population.* Washington, DC: Government Printing Office, 1902.

—. *Mortality Statistics, 1900 to 1904.* Washington, DC: Government Printing Office, 1906.

—. *Insane and Feeble-Minded in Institutions, 1910.* Washington, DC: Government Printing Office, 1914.

—. *Mortality Rates, 1910–1920.* Washington, DC: Government Printing Office, 1922.

—. *Historical Statistics of the United States, Colonial Times to 1970.* 2 vols. Washington, DC: Government Printing Office, 1975.

—. *Measuring America: The Decennial Censuses from 1790 to 2000.* Washington, DC: US Census Bureau, 2002.

US Pension Bureau. *Instructions to Examining Surgeons for Pensions.* Washington, DC: Government Printing Office, 1887.

US Pension Office. *Instructions to Examining Surgeons for Pensions.* Washington, DC: Government Printing Office, 1884.

—. *Instructions to Examining Surgeons of the Bureau of Pensions.* Washington, DC: Government Printing Office, 1893.

Walker, Francis A. *The Statistics of the Population of the United States...from the Original Returns of the Ninth Census.* Washington, DC: Government Printing Office, 1872.

Wines, Frederick H. *Report on the Defective, Dependent, and Delinquent Classes.* Washington, DC: Government Printing Office, 1888.

Published Primary Sources

American Psychiatric Association. *Diagnostic and Statistical Manual of Mental Disorders.* 5th ed. Arlington, VA: American Psychiatric Association, 2013.

Beard, George M. *American Nervousness, Its Causes and Consequences.* New York: G. P. Putnam, 1881.

Bennett, Edwin C. *Musket and Sword, or the Camp, March, and Firing Line of the Army of the Potomac.* Boston: Coburn, 1900.

Bibliography

Berlin, Ira, Joseph F. Reidy, and Leslie S. Rowland, eds. *Freedom: A Documentary History of Emancipation: Series II. The Black Military Experience*. New York: Cambridge University Press, 1982.

Bruce, Philip A. *The Plantation Negro as a Freeman*. New York: G. P. Putnam, 1889.

Clark, William. "Alcohol for Soldiers." *Army and Navy Register*, June 4, 1900.

Clevenger, S. V. *Spinal Concussion*. Philadelphia: F. A. Davis, 1889.

Da Costa, J. M. "On Irritable Heart: A Clinical Study of a Form of Functional Cardiac Disorder and Its Consequences." *American Journal of Medical Sciences* 61 (1871), 17–52.

Dollard, Robert. *Recollections of the Civil War and Going West to Grow Up with the Country*. Scotland, SD: Robert Dollard, 1906.

Hoffman, Frederick L. "Race Traits and Tendencies of the American Negro." *Publications of the American Economic Association* 11 (1896), 126.

Howle, W. C. "The Drink Habit." *Journal of the American Medical Association* 19 (1892), 575.

Journal of the Twenty-Fourth Annual Session of the National Encampment, Grand Army of the Republic. Detroit, MI: Richmond and Backus, 1890.

Mathews, William. "Civilization and Suicide." *North American Review* 152 (1891), 470–485.

Miller, J. F. "The Effects of Emancipation upon the Mental and Physical Health of the Negro of the South." *North Carolina Medical Journal* 38 (1896), 285–294.

Morselli, Enrico. *Suicide: An Essay on Comparative Moral Statistics*. New York: D. Appleton, 1882.

Murlin, Edgar L. *The New York Red Book*. Albany, NY: James B. Lyon, 1897.

Murray, George W. *A History of George W. Murray and His Long Confinement in Andersonville, Ga.* Northampton, MA: Trumbull and Gere, 1860.

Nagle, John T. *Suicides in New York City during the Eleven Years Ending Dec. 31, 1880*. Cambridge, MA: Riverside, 1882.

Pollard, E. A. *Southern History of the War*. New York: Charles R. Richardson, 1866.

Porter, Horace P. "The Common Nervous Trouble of Old Soldiers." *Leonard's Illustrated Medical Journal* 10 (1889), 22.

Powell, Theophilus O. "The Increase of Insanity and Tuberculosis in the Southern Negro since 1860." *Journal of the American Medical Association* 26 (1896), 1185–1186.

Schouler, William. *History of Massachusetts in the Civil War*. 2 vols. Boston: William Schouler, 1871.

Stearns, I. H. "A New Name for an Old Veteran's Disease." *Medical Summary* 10 (1888), 49–50.

Newspapers

Baltimore Sun
Barnstable Patriot
Beverly Citizen
Boston Advertiser
Boston Courier
Boston Globe
Boston Herald
Boston Journal
Boston Post
Boston Transcript
Boston Traveler
Christian Recorder
Hamilton [OH] *Journal*
Indianapolis Journal
Lowell Citizen
Macon [GA] *Telegraph*
[Worcester] *Massachusetts Spy*
Newark Advertiser
New Haven Reporter
New York Herald
New York Sun
New York Times

Bibliography

New York World
Omaha Bee
Palatka [FL] *News*
Springfield [MA] *Republican*

Digitized Data Sources

Center for Population Economics, University of Chicago. Survivors of Andersonville Prison, http://uadata.org.

Centers for Disease Control and Prevention. National Violent Death Reporting System, www.cdc.gov/injury/wisqars/nvdrs.html.

Costa, Dora L., Robert W. Fogel, Louis Cain, Sok Chul Hong, Sven Wilson, Louis Nguyen, Joseph Burton, and Noelle Yetter. *The Aging of US Colored Troops*. Chicago: Center for Population Economics, University of Chicago, 2015, http://uadata.org.

Fogel, Robert W., Dora L. Costa, Hoyt Bleakley, Louis Cain, Sok Chul Hong, Chulhee Lee, Sven Wilson, Louis Nguyen, Joseph Burton, Noelle Yetter, and Carlos Villarreal. *The Impact of Urban Disparities on Aging and Mortality*. Chicago: Center for Population Economics, University of Chicago, 2015, http://uadata.org.

Fogel, Robert W., Dora L. Costa, Michael Haines, Chulhee Lee, Louis Nguyen, Clayne Pope, Irvin Rosenberg, Nevin Scrimshaw, James Trussell, Sven Wilson, Larry T. Wimmer, John Kim, Julene Bassett, Joseph Burton, and Noelle Yetter. *Aging of Veterans of the Union Army: Version M-5*. Chicago: Center for Population Economics, University of Chicago, 2000, http://uadata.org.

Fogel, Robert W., Dora L. Costa, Sven Wilson, Chulhee Lee, Louis Nguyen, Joseph Burton, and Noelle Yetter. *The Aging of US Colored Troops*. Chicago: Center for Population Economics, University of Chicago, 2004, http://uadata.org.

Historical Data Systems, Inc. US Civil War Soldier Records and Profiles, 1861–1865, http://search.ancestry.com/search/db.aspx?dbid=1138.

Ruggles, Steven, Katie Genadek, Ronald Goeken, Josiah Grover, and Matthew Sobek. *Integrated Public Use Microdata Series: Version 6.0*. Minneapolis: University of Minnesota, 2015, www.ipums.org.

US Department of Veterans Affairs, Veteran Population Projection Model 2014, www.va.gov/vetdata/Veteran_Population.asp.

Secondary Sources

Abbott, Edith. "The Civil War and the Crime Wave of 1865–1870." *Social Service Review* 1 (1927), 212–234.

Adams, John G. B. "The Massachusetts Soldiers' Home." *New England Magazine* 6 (1890), 689–698.

Adams, Michael C. C. *Living Hell: The Dark Side of the Civil War*. Baltimore: Johns Hopkins University Press, 2014.

Anderson, David. "Dying of Nostalgia: Homesickness in the Union Army during the Civil War." *Civil War History* 56 (2010), 247–282.

Anderson, Olive. "Did Suicide Increase with Industrialization in Victorian England?" *Past and Present* 86 (1980), 149–173.

—. *Suicide in Victorian and Edwardian England*. New York: Oxford University Press, 1987.

Andrews, Bernice, Chris R. Brewin, Rosanna Philpott, and Lorna Stewart. "Delayed-Onset Posttraumatic Stress Disorder: A Systematic Review of the Evidence." *American Journal of Psychiatry* 164 (2007), 1319–1326.

Bailey, Victor. *"This Rash Act": Suicide across the Life Cycle in the Victorian City*. Stanford, CA: Stanford University Press, 1998.

Barton, Michael, and Larry M. Logue. "The Soldiers and the Scholars." In *The Civil War Soldier: A Historical Reader*, edited by Michael Barton and Larry M. Logue, 1–5. New York: New York University Press, 2002.

Bell, Richard. *We Shall Be No More: Suicide and Self-Government in the Newly United States*. Cambridge, MA: Harvard University Press, 2012.

Billings, John S. "The Health of the Survivors of the War." *Forum* 12 (1891–92), 652–658.

Blake, Kellee. "'First in the Path of the Firemen': The Fate of the 1890 Population Census." *Prologue* 28 (1996), 168–181.

Blanck, Peter. "Civil War Pensions and Disability." *Ohio State Law Review* 62 (2001), 109–238.

Bibliography

Blight, David W. *Race and Reunion: The Civil War in American Memory*. Cambridge, MA: Harvard University Press, 2001.

Bracken, Patrick J. "Post-Modernity and Post-Traumatic Stress Disorder." *Social Science and Medicine* 53 (2001), 733–743.

Bradley, Mark A. *Bluecoats and Tar Heels: Soldiers and Civilians in Reconstruction North Carolina*. Lexington: University Press of Kentucky, 2009.

Brenner, Lisa A., Lisa M. Betthauser, Beeta Y. Homaifar, Edgar Villarreal, Jeri E. F. Harwood, Pamela J. Staves, and Joseph A. Huggins. "Posttraumatic Stress Disorder, Traumatic Brain Injury, and Suicide Attempt History among Veterans Receiving Mental Health Services." *Suicide and Life-Threatening Behavior* 41 (2011), 416–423.

Brian, Kathleen M. "'The Weight of Perhaps Ten or a Dozen Human Lives': Suicide, Accountability, and the Life-Saving Technologies of the Asylum." *Bulletin of the History of Medicine* 90 (2016), 583–610.

Brock, Rita N., and Gabriella Lettini. *Soul Repair: Recovering from Moral Injury After War*. Boston: Beacon, 2012.

Buck, Steven J. "'A Contest in Which Blood Must Flow like Water': Du Page County and the Civil War." *Illinois Historical Journal* 87 (1994), 2–20.

Bussanich, Leonard. "'Will I Ever Be Fit for Civil Society Again?' The Challenges of Readjustment through the Prism of the New Jersey Soldier's Home at Newark." *New Jersey History* 127 (2013), n.p.

Chamberlin, Sheena M. E. "Emasculated by Trauma: A Social History of Post-Traumatic Stress Disorder, Stigma, and Masculinity." *Journal of American Culture* 35 (2012), 358–365.

Christ, Mark K., ed. *"All Cut to Pieces and Gone to Hell": The Civil War, Race Relations, and the Battle of Poison Spring*. Little Rock, AR: August House, 2003.

Cimbala, Paul A. *Veterans North and South: The Transition from Soldier to Civilian after the American Civil War*. Santa Barbara, CA: Praeger, 2015.

Cimprich, John. *Fort Pillow, a Civil War Massacre, and Public Memory*. Baton Rouge: Louisiana State University Press, 2011.

Cirillo, Vincent J. "Two Faces of Death: Fatalities from Disease and Combat in America's Principal Wars, 1775 to Present." *Perspectives in Biology and Medicine* 51 (2008), 121–133.

Clarke, Frances. "So Lonesome I Could Die: Nostalgia and Debates over Emotional Control in the Civil War North." *Journal of Social History* 41 (2007), 253–282.

Cloyd, Benjamin G. *Haunted by Atrocity: Civil War Prisons in American Memory*. Baton Rouge: Louisiana State University Press, 2010.

Coleman, Loren. *The Copycat Effect: How the Media and Popular Culture Trigger the Mayhem of Tomorrow's Headlines*. New York: Simon and Schuster, 2004.

Condran, Gretchen A., and Eileen Crimmins. "A Description and Evaluation of Mortality Data in the Federal Census: 1850–1900." *Historical Methods* 12 (1979), 1–23.

Conk, Margo A. "Occupational Classification in the United States Census: 1870–1940." *Journal of Interdisciplinary History* 9 (1978), 111–130.

Cook, Robert. "The Quarrel Forgotten? Toward a Clearer Understanding of Sectional Reconciliation." *Journal of the Civil War Era* 6 (2016), 413–436.

Costa, Dora L., and Matthew E. Kahn. "Forging a New Identity: The Costs and Benefits of Diversity in Civil War Combat Units for Black Slaves and Freemen." *Journal of Economic History* 66 (2006), 936–962.

—. "Surviving Andersonville: The Benefits of Social Networks in POW Camps." *American Economic Review* 97 (2007), 1467–1487.

—. "Health, Wartime Stress, and Unit Cohesion: Evidence from Union Army Veterans." *Demography* 47 (2010), 45–66.

—. *Heroes and Cowards: The Social Face of War*. Princeton, NJ: Princeton University Press, 2010.

Costa, Dora L., Heather DeSomer, Eric Hanss, Christopher Roudiez, Sven E. Wilson, and Noelle Yetter. "Union Army Veterans, All Grown Up." *Historical Methods* 50 (2017), 79–95.

Cushman, John H., Jr., and Tom Shanker. "A War Like No Other Uses New 21st-Century Methods to Disable Enemy Forces." New York Times, April 10, 2003.

Bibliography

Danigelis, Nick, and Whitney Pope. "Durkheim's Theory of Suicide as Applied to the Family: An Empirical Test." *Social Forces* 57 (1979), 1081–1106.

Davidson, Jonathan R. T., Harold S. Kudler, William B. Saunders, and Rebecca D. Smith. "Symptom and Comorbidity Patterns in World War II and Vietnam Veterans with Posttraumatic Stress Disorder." *Comprehensive Psychiatry* 31 (1990), 162–170.

Dayton, Cornelia H. "'The Oddest Man That I Ever Saw': Assessing Cognitive Disability on Eighteenth-Century Cape Cod." *Journal of Social History* 49 (2015), 77–99.

Dean, Eric T., Jr. *Shook over Hell: Post-Traumatic Stress, Vietnam, and the Civil War*. Cambridge, MA: Harvard University Press, 1997.

—. "Reflections on 'The Trauma of War' and *Shook over Hell*." *Civil War History* 59 (2013), 414–418.

Douglas, Jack D. *The Social Meanings of Suicide*. Princeton, NJ: Princeton University Press, 1967.

Downs, Gregory P. *After Appomattox: Military Occupation and the Ends of War*. Cambridge, MA: Harvard University Press, 2015.

Dreazen, Yochi. *The Invisible Front: Love and Loss in an Era of Endless War*. New York: Crown, 2014.

Drescher, Kent D., David W. Foy, Caroline Kelly, Anna Leshner, Kerrie Schutz, and Brett Litz. "An Exploration of the Viability and Usefulness of the Construct of Moral Injury in War Veterans." *Traumatology* 17 (2011), 8–13.

Duncan, Russell, and David J. Klooster, eds. *Phantoms of a Blood-Stained Period: The Complete Civil War Writings of Ambrose Bierce*. Amherst: University of Massachusetts Press, 2002.

Durkheim, Émile. *Suicide: A Study in Sociology*. Trans. John A. Spaulding and George Simpson. Glencoe, IL: Free Press, 1951.

Durrill, Wayne K. *War of Another Kind: A Southern Community in the Great Rebellion*. New York: Oxford University Press, 1990.

Eckberg, Douglas Lee. "Stalking the Elusive Homicide: A Capture–Recapture Approach to the Estimation of Post-Reconstruction South Carolina Killings." *Social Science History* 25 (2001), 67–91.

Elder, Gregory A. "Update on TBI and Cognitive Impairment in Military Veterans." *Current Neurology and Neuroscience Reports* 15 (2015), 1–9.

Faust, Drew G. *This Republic of Suffering: Death and the American Civil War*. New York: Knopf, 2008.

Franklin, Joseph C., Jessica D. Ribeiro, Kathryn R. Fox, Kate H. Bentley, Evan M. Kleiman, Xieyining Huang, Katherine M. Musacchio, Adam C. Jaroszewski, Bernard P. Chang, and Matthew K. Nock. "Risk Factors for Suicidal Thoughts and Behaviors: A Meta-Analysis of 50 Years of Research." *Psychological Bulletin* 143 (2017), 187–232.

Friedman, Matthew J. "Veterans' Mental Health in the Wake of War." *New England Journal of Medicine* 352 (2005), 1287–1290.

Frueh, B. Christopher, and Jeffrey A. Smith. "Suicide, Alcoholism, and Psychiatric Illness among Union Forces during the US Civil War." *Journal of Anxiety Disorders* 26 (2012), 769–775.

Gade, Daniel M. "A Better Way to Help Veterans." *National Affairs* 16 (2013), 58.

Gajda, Amy. "What If Samuel D. Warren Hadn't Married a Senator's Daughter? Uncovering the Press Coverage That Led to 'The Right to Privacy.'" *Michigan State Law Review* 35 (2008), 35–60.

Gallagher, Gary W., and Kathryn Shively Meier. "Coming to Terms with Civil War Military History." *Journal of the Civil War Era* 4 (2014), 492.

Gallman, J. Matthew. "In Your Hands That Musket Means Liberty: African American Soldiers and the Battle of Olustee." In Joan Waugh and Gary W. Gallagher, eds., *Wars within a War: Controversy and Conflict over the American Civil War*. Chapel Hill: University of North Carolina Press, 2009.

Gannon, Barbara. *The Won Cause: Black and White Comradeship in the Grand Army of the Republic*. Chapel Hill: University of North Carolina Press, 2011.

Gibbons, Robert D. C., Hendricks Brown, and Kwan Hur. "Is the Rate of Suicide among Veterans Elevated?" *American Journal of Public Health* 102 (2012), S17–S19.

Glasson, William Henry. *Federal Military Pensions in the United States*. New York: Oxford University Press, 1918.

Bibliography

Glatthaar, Joseph. *Forged in Battle: The Civil War Alliance of Black Soldiers and White Officers*. New York: Free Press, 1990.

Grob, Gerald N. *The Mad among Us: A History of the Care of America's Mentally Ill*. New York: Simon and Schuster, 1994.

—. *The Deadly Truth: A History of Disease in America*. Cambridge, MA: Harvard University Press, 2009.

Gutman, Robert. "The Accuracy of Vital Statistics in Massachusetts, 1842–1901." PhD diss., Columbia University, 1956.

—. "Birth and Death Registration in Massachusetts, II: The Inauguration of a Modern System, 1800–1849." *Milbank Memorial Fund Quarterly* 36 (1958), 373–402.

—. "Birth and Death Registration in Massachusetts, III: The System Achieves a Form, 1849–1869." *Milbank Memorial Fund Quarterly* 37 (1959), 309–326.

Hacker, J. David. "Decennial Life Tables for the White Population of the United States, 1790–1900." *Historical Methods* 43 (2010), 45–79.

—. "New Estimates of Census Coverage in the United States, 1850–1930." *Social Science History* 37 (2013), 71–101.

Hacking, Ian. *Rewriting the Soul: Multiple Personality and the Sciences of Memory*. Princeton, NJ: Princeton University Press, 1995.

—. *Mad Travelers: Reflections on the Reality of Transient Mental Illnesses*. Charlottesville: University Press of Virginia, 1998.

Haines, Michael R. "Estimated Life Tables for the United States, 1850–1910." *Historical Methods* 31 (1998), 149–169.

Handley-Cousins, Sarah. "'Wrestling at the Gates of Death': Joshua Lawrence Chamberlain and Nonvisible Disability in the Post–Civil War North." *Journal of the Civil War Era* 6 (2016), 220–242.

Hanna, William F. "The Boston Draft Riot." *Civil War History* 36 (1990). 262–273.

Harrington, Ralph. "On the Tracks of Trauma: Railway Spine Reconsidered." *Social History of Medicine* 16 (2003), 209–223.

Healy, Róisín. "Suicide in Early Modern and Modern Europe." *Historical Journal* 49 (2006), 906.

Hess, Earl J. *The Union Soldier in Battle: Enduring the Ordeal of Combat*. Lawrence: University Press of Kansas, 1997.

Horwitz, Tony. "The Civil War's Hidden Legacy." *Smithsonian* 45 (2015), 44–49.

Houston, Rab. "Fact, Truth, and the Limits of Sympathy: Newspaper Reporting of Suicide in the North of England, circa 1750–1830." *Studies in the Literary Imagination* 44 (2011), 93–108.

Hsieh, Wayne Wei-Siang. "'Go to Your Gawd Like a Soldier': Transnational Reflections on Veteranhood." *Journal of the Civil War Era* 5 (2015), 551–577.

Hughes, John S. "Labeling and Treating Black Mental Illness in Alabama, 1861–1910." *Journal of Southern History* 58 (1992), 435–460.

Humphreys, Margaret. *Marrow of Tragedy: The Health Crisis of the American Civil War*. Baltimore, MD: Johns Hopkins University Press, 2013.

Hyams, Kenneth C., F. Stephen Wignall, and Robert Roswell. "War Syndromes and Their Evaluation: From the US Civil War to the Persian Gulf War." *Annals of Internal Medicine* 125 (1996), 398–405.

Jackson, James C., Patricia L. Sinnott, Brian P. Marx, Maureen Murdoch, Nina A. Sayer, JoAnn M. Alvarez, Robert A. Greevy, Paula P. Schnurr, Matthew J. Friedman, Andrea C. Shane, Richard R. Owen, Terence M. Keane, and Theodore Speroff. "Variation in Practices and Attitudes of Clinicians Assessing PTSD-Related Disability among Veterans." *Journal of Traumatic Stress*, 24 (2011), 609–613.

Janney, Caroline E.*Remembering the Civil War: Reunion and the Limits of Reconciliation*. Chapel Hill: University of North Carolina Press, 2013.

Jentzen, Jeffrey M. *Death Investigation in America: Coroners, Medical Examiners, and the Pursuit of Medical Certainty*. Cambridge, MA: Harvard University Press, 2009.

Johnson, Russell L. "The Civil War Generation: Military Service and Mobility in Dubuque, Iowa, 1860–1870." *Journal of Social History* 32 (1999), 791–820.

Johnson, Walter. "On Agency." *Journal of Social History* 37 (2003), 113–124.

Bibliography

—. "Agency: A Ghost Story." In Richard Follett, Eric Foner, and Walter Johnson, eds., *Slavery's Ghosts: The Problem of Freedom in the Age of Emancipation*. Baltimore: Johns Hopkins University Press, 2011.

Jordan, Brian Matthew. *Marching Home: Union Veterans and Their Unending Civil War*. New York: Liveright, 2015.

—. "'Our Work Is Not Yet Finished': Union Veterans and Their Unending Civil War, 1865–1872." *Journal of the Civil War Era* 5 (2015), 484–503.

Kelly, Patrick J. *Creating a National Home: Building the Veterans' Welfare State, 1860–1900*. Cambridge, MA: Harvard University Press, 1997.

Kemp, Thomas R. "Community and War: The Experience of Two New Hampshire Towns." In Maris A. Vinovskis, ed., *Toward a Social History of the American Civil War: Exploratory Essays*. New York: Cambridge University Press, 1990.

Keyssar, Alexander. *Out of Work: The First Century of Unemployment in Massachusetts*. New York: Cambridge University Press, 1986.

Kim, Hyungjin, Eric G. Smith, Dara Ganoczy, Heather Walters, Clare M. Stano, Mark A. Ilgen, Amy S. B. Bohnert, and Marcia Valenstein. "Predictors of Suicide in Patient Charts among Patients with Depression in the Veterans Administration Health System: Importance of Prescription Drug and Alcohol Abuse." *Journal of Clinical Psychiatry* 73 (2012), 1260–1275.

Kposowa, Augustine J., K. D. Breault, and Gopal K. Singh. "White Male Suicide in the United States: A Multivariate Individual-Level Analysis." *Social Forces* 74 (1995), 315–323.

Kreiser, Lawrence A., Jr. "A Socioeconomic Study of Veterans of the 103rd Ohio Volunteer Infantry Regiment after the Civil War." *Ohio History* 107 (1998), 171–184.

Kulka, Richard A., William E. Schlenger, John A. Fairbank, Richard L. Hough, B. Kathleen Jordan, Charles R. Marmar, and Daniel S. Weiss. *Trauma and the Vietnam War Generation: Report of Findings from the National Vietnam Veterans Readjustment Study*. New York: Brunner Mazel, 1990.

Kushner, Howard I. *Self-Destruction in the Promised Land: A Psycho-cultural Biology of American Suicide*. New Brunswick, NJ: Rutgers University Press, 1989.

—. "Suicide, Gender, and the Fear of Modernity in Nineteenth-Century Medical and Social Thought." *Journal of Social History* 26 (1993), 461–490.

Lainhart, Ann S. *State Census Records*. Baltimore: Genealogical Publishing, 1991.

Lande, R. Gregory. "Felo De Se: Soldier Suicides in America's Civil War." *Military Medicine* 176 (2011), 531–536.

Lane, Roger. *Violent Death in the City: Suicide, Accident, and Murder in Nineteenth-Century Philadelphia*. Cambridge, MA: Harvard University Press, 1979.

Lee, Chulhee. "Wealth Accumulation and the Health of Union Army Veterans, 1860–1870." *Journal of Economic History* 65 (2005), 352–385.

Lender, Mark E., and James K. Martin. *Drinking in America: A History*. New York: Simon and Schuster, 1987.

Lerner, Paul. "From Traumatic Neurosis to Male Hysteria: The Decline and Fall of Hermann Oppenheim, 1889–1919." In Mark S. Micale and Paul Lerner, eds., *Traumatic Pasts: History, Psychiatry, and Trauma in the Modern Age, 1870–1930*. New York: Cambridge University Press, 2001.

Lester, David, and Bijou Yang. "The Influence of War on Suicide Rates." *Journal of Social Psychology* 132 (1992), 135–137.

Linderman, Gerald F. *Embattled Courage: The Experience of Combat in the American Civil War*. New York: Free Press, 1987.

Litz, Brett T., Nathan Stein, Eileen Delaney, Leslie Lebowitz, William P. Nash, Caroline Silva, and Shira Maguen. "Moral Injury and Moral Repair in War Veterans: A Preliminary Model and Intervention Strategy." *Clinical Psychological Review* 29 (2009), 695–706.

Logue, Larry M. "Confederate Survivors and the 'Civil War Question' in the 1910 Census." *Historical Methods* 34 (2001), 89–93.

—. "Elephants and Epistemology: Evidence of Suicide in the Gilded Age." *Journal of Social History* 49 (2015), 374–386.

Bibliography

Logue, Larry M., and Michael Barton. *The Civil War Veteran: A Historical Reader*. New York: New York University Press, 2007.

Logue, Larry M., and Peter Blanck. *Race, Ethnicity, and Disability: Veterans and Benefits in Post–Civil War America*. New York: Cambridge University Press, 2010.

Loughran, Tracey. "Shell Shock, Trauma, and the First World War: The Making of a Diagnosis and Its Histories." *Journal of the History of Medicine and the Allied Sciences* 67 (2010), 94–119.

McClurken, Jeffrey W. *Take Care of the Living: Reconstructing Confederate Veteran Families in Virginia*. Charlottesville: University Virginia Press, 2009.

McConnell, Stuart. *Glorious Contentment: The Grand Army of the Republic, 1865–1900*. Chapel Hill: University of North Carolina Press, 1992.

McCormick-Goodhart, Mark A. "Leaving No Veteran Behind: Policies and Perspectives on Combat Trauma, Veterans Courts, and the Rehabilitative Approach to Criminal Behavior." *Penn State Law Review* 125 (2012), 895–926.

MacDonald, Michael, and Terence R. Murphy. *Sleepless Souls: Suicide in Early Modern England*. New York: Oxford University Press, 1993.

McHugh, Paul R., and Glenn Treisman. "PTSD: A Problematic Diagnostic Category." *Journal of Anxiety Disorders* 21 (2007), 220–221.

McNally, Richard J. "Progress and Controversy in the Study of Posttraumatic Stress Disorder." *Annual Review of Psychology* 54 (2003), 229–252.

McNally, Richard J., and B. Christopher Frueh. "Why Are Iraq and Afghanistan War Veterans Seeking PTSD Disability Compensation at Unprecedented Rates?" *Journal of Anxiety Disorders* 27 (2013), 520–526.

Marmar, Charles R., William Schlenger, and Clare Henn-Haase. "Course of Posttraumatic Stress Disorder 40 Years after the Vietnam War: Findings from the National Vietnam Veterans Longitudinal Study." *JAMA Psychiatry* 72 (2015), 875–881.

Marshall, James R. "Political Integration and the Effect of War on Suicide: United States, 1933–76." *Social Forces* 59 (1981), 771–785.

Marten, James. *Sing Not War: The Lives of Union and Confederate Veterans in Gilded Age America*. Chapel Hill: University of North Carolina Press, 2011.

Marvel, William. *Andersonville: The Last Depot*. Chapel Hill: University of North Carolina Press, 1994.

Mays, Thomas D. "The Battle of Saltville." In John David Smith, ed., *Black Soldiers in Blue: African American Troops in the Civil War Era*. Chapel Hill: University of North Carolina Press, 2002.

Meier, Kathryn S. *Nature's Civil War: Common Soldiers and the Environment in 1862 Virginia*. Chapel Hill: University of North Carolina Press, 2013.

Meyer, Jessica. "Separating the Men from the Boys: Masculinity and Maturity in Understandings of Shell Shock in Britain." *Twentieth Century British History* 20 (2009), 1–22.

Miller, Brian Craig. *Empty Sleeves: Amputation in the Civil War South*. Athens: University of Georgia Press, 2015.

—. "A Song for the Suffering: The Interminable Civil War." *South Central Review* 33 (2016), 53–68.

Mitchell, Reid. "'Not the General but the Soldier': The Study of Civil War Soldiers." In James M. McPherson and William J. Cooper, eds., *Writing the Civil War: The Quest to Understand*. Columbia: University of South Carolina Press, 1998.

Mittal, Dinesh, Karen L. Drummond, Dean Blevins, Geoffrey Curran, Patrick Corrigan, and Greer Sullivan. "Stigma Associated with PTSD: Perceptions of Treatment Seeking Combat Veterans." *Psychiatric Rehabilitation Journal* 36 (2013), 86–92.

Mohr, James C. *Doctors and the Law: Medical Jurisprudence in Nineteenth-Century America*. Baltimore: Johns Hopkins University Press, 1996.

Monkkonen, Eric H. *Murder in New York City*. Berkeley: University of California Press, 2001.

Nelson, Megan Kate. *Ruin Nation: Destruction and the American Civil War*. Athens: University of Georgia Press, 2012.

Nielssen, Olav, Duncan Wallace, and Matthew Large. "Pokorny's Complaint: The Insoluble Problem of the Overwhelming Number of False

Positives Generated by Suicide Risk Assessment." *BJPsych Bulletin* 41 (2017), 18–20.

O'Connor, Thomas H. *Civil War Boston: Homefront and Battlefield*. Boston: Northeastern University Press, 1997.

Okie, Susan. "Traumatic Brain Injury in the War Zone." *New England Journal of Medicine* 352 (2005), 2043–2047.

Padilla, Jalyn O. "Army of 'Cripples': Northern Civil War Amputees, Disability, and Manhood in Victorian America." PhD diss., University of Delaware, 2007.

Pettegrew, John. "'The Soldier's Faith': Turn-of-the-Century Memory of the Civil War and the Emergence of Modern American Nationalism." *Journal of Contemporary History* 31 (1996), 49–73.

Philipps, Dave. "A Unit Stalked by Suicide, Trying to Save Itself." *New York Times*, September 20, 2015.

—. "Suicide Rate among Veterans Has Risen Sharply since 2001." *New York Times*, July 7, 2016.

Pizarro, Judith, Roxane Cohen Silver, and JoAnn Prause. "Physical and Mental Health Costs of Traumatic War Experiences among Civil War Veterans." *Archives of General Psychiatry* 63 (2006), 193–200.

Prechtel-Kluskens, Claire. "'A Reasonable Degree of Promptitude': Civil War Pension Application Processing, 1861–1885." *Prologue* 42 (2010), 26–35.

Reardon, Carol. "Writing Battle History: The Challenge of Memory." *Civil War History* 53 (2007), 252–263.

Richardson, Lisa K., B. Christopher Frueh, and Ronald Acierno. "Prevalence Estimates of Combat-Related Post-Traumatic Stress Disorder: Critical Review." *Australian and New Zealand Journal of Psychiatry* 44 (2010), 4–19.

Reger, Mark A., Derek J. Smolenski, Nancy A. Skopp, Melinda J. Metzger-Abamukang, Han K. Kang, Tim A. Bullman, Sondra Perdue, and Gregory A. Gahm. "Risk of Suicide among US Military Service Members Following Operation Enduring Freedom or Operation Iraqi Freedom Deployment and Separation from the US Military." *JAMA Psychiatry* 72 (2015), 561–569.

Reid, Richard. "USCT Veterans in Post–Civil War North Carolina." In John David Smith, ed., *Black Soldiers in Blue: African American*

Troops in the Civil War Era. Chapel Hill: University of North Carolina Press, 2002.

—. *Freedom for Themselves: North Carolina's Black Soldiers in the Civil War Era*. Chapel Hill: University of North Carolina Press, 2012.

Roelfs, David, Eran Shor, Karina Davidson, and Joseph Schwartz. "War-Related Stress and Mortality: A Meta-Analysis." *International Journal of Epidemiology* 39 (2010), 1499–1509.

Rorabaugh, W. J. "Who Fought for the North in the Civil War? Concord, Massachusetts, Enlistments." *Journal of American History* 73 (1986), 695–701.

Rosen, Hannah. *Terror in the Heart of Freedom: Citizenship, Sexual Violence, and the Meaning of Race in the Postemancipation South*. Chapel Hill: University of North Carolina Press, 2009.

Rosenbaum, Betty B. "Relationship between War and Crime in the United States." *Journal of Criminal Law and Criminology* 30 (1940), 722–740.

Rothman, Sheila M. *Living in the Shadow of Death: Tuberculosis and the Social Experience of Illness in American History*. New York: Basic Books, 1994.

Rugh, Susan S. "'Awful Calamities Now upon Us': The Civil War in Fountain Green, Illinois." *Journal of the Illinois State Historical Society* 93 (2000), 9–42.

Rutter, Michael. "Resilience as a Dynamic Concept." *Development and Psychopathology* 24 (2012), 335–344.

Sayer, Nina A., Greta Friedemann-Sanchez, Michele Spoont, Maureen Murdoch, Louise E. Parker, Christine Chiros, and Robert Rosenheck. "A Qualitative Study of Determinants of PTSD Treatment Initiation in Veterans." *Psychiatry* 72 (2009), 238–255.

Schaefer, Michael W. "'Really, Though, I'm Fine': Civil War Veterans and the Psychological Aftereffects of Killing." In Lawrence A. Kreiser and Randal Allred, eds., *The Civil War in Popular Culture: Memory and Meaning*. Lexington: University Press of Kentucky, 2014.

Schantz, Mark S. *Awaiting the Heavenly Country: The Civil War and America's Culture of Death*. Ithaca, NY: Cornell University Press, 2008.

Sekar, C. Chandra, and W. Edwards Deming. "On a Method of Estimating Birth and Death Rates and the Extent of Registration." *Journal of the American Statistical Association* 44 (1949), 101–115.

Shaffer, Donald R. *After the Glory: The Struggles of Black Civil War Veterans*. Lawrence: University Press of Kansas, 2004.

Shaw, Kathleen. "'Johnny Has Gone for a Soldier': Youth Enlistment in a Northern County." *Pennsylvania Magazine of History and Biography* 135 (2011), 419–446.

Shay, Jonathan. *Achilles in Vietnam: Combat Trauma and the Undoing of Character*. New York: Scribner, 1994.

Sheehan-Dean, Aaron. "The Blue and the Gray in Black and White: Assessing the Scholarship on Civil War Soldiers." In Aaron Sheehan-Dean, ed., *The View from the Ground: Experiences of Civil War Soldiers*. Lexington: University Press of Kentucky, 2007.

Shively, Sharon B., and Daniel P. Perl. "Traumatic Brain Injury, Shell Shock, and Posttraumatic Stress Disorder in the Military – Past, Present, and Future." *Journal of Head Trauma Rehabilitation* 27 (2012), 234–239.

Sicherman, Barbara. "The Uses of a Diagnosis: Doctors, Patients, and Neurasthenia." *Journal of the History of Medicine and Allied Sciences* 32 (1977), 33–54.

Silkenat, David. *Moments of Despair: Suicide, Divorce, and Debt in Civil War Era North Carolina*. Chapel Hill: University of North Carolina Press, 2011.

Skocpol, Theda. *Protecting Soldiers and Mothers: The Political Origins of Social Policy in the United States*. Cambridge, MA: Harvard University Press, 1992.

Smith, John David. *Black Judas: William Hannibal Thomas and the American Negro*. Athens: University of Georgia Press, 2000.

—. "Let Us All Be Grateful That We Have Colored Troops That Will Fight." In John David Smith, ed., *Black Soldiers in Blue: African American Troops in the Civil War Era*. Chapel Hill: University of North Carolina Press, 2005.

Smith, Tyler C., Margaret A. K. Ryan, Deborah L. Wingard, Donald J. Slymen, James F. Sallis, and Donna Kritz-Silverstein. "New Onset and Persistent Symptoms of Post-Traumatic Stress Disorder

Self Reported after Deployment and Combat Exposures: Prospective Population Based US Military Cohort Study." *British Medical Journal* 336 (2008), 366–371.

Smith-Rosenberg, Carroll. "The Hysterical Woman: Sex Roles and Role Conflict in 19th-Century America." *Social Research* 39 (1972), 652–678.

Snell, Mark A. "'If They Would Know What I Know It Would be Pretty Hard to Raise One Company in York': Recruiting, the Draft, and Society's Response in York County, Pennsylvania, 1861–1865." In Paul A. Cimbala and Randall M. Miller, eds., *Union Soldiers and the Northern Home Front: Wartime Experiences, Postwar Adjustments*. New York: Fordham University Press, 2002.

Somers, Howard, and Jean Somers. "On Losing a Veteran Son to a Broken System." *New York Times*, November 11, 2013.

Sommerville, Diane M. "'Will They Ever Be Able to Forget?': Confederate Soldiers and Mental Illness in the Defeated South." In Stephen Berry, ed., *Weirding the War: Stories from the Civil War's Ragged Edges*. Athens: University of Georgia Press, 2011.

—. "'A Burden Too Heavy to Bear': War Trauma, Suicide, and Confederate Soldiers." *Civil War History* 59 (2013), 453–491.

Stack, Steven. "Suicide: A 15-Year Review of the Sociological Literature – Part II: Modernization and the Social Integration Perspectives." *Suicide and Life-Threatening Behavior* 30 (2000), 163–176.

Starr, Paul. *The Creation of the Media: Political Origins of Modern Communications*. New York: Basic Books, 2004.

Steckel, Richard H. "Census Manuscript Schedules Matched with Property Tax Lists." *Historical Methods* 27 (1994), 71–86.

Sternhell, Yael A. "Revisionism Reinvented? The Antiwar Turn in Civil War Scholarship." *Journal of the Civil War Era* 3 (2013), 239–256.

Sturges, Michael. "Post-Traumatic Stress Disorder in the Civil War: Connecticut Casualties and a Look into the Mind." In Matthew Warshauer, ed., *Inside Connecticut and the Civil War: Essays on One State's Struggles*. Middletown, CT: Wesleyan University Press, 2013.

Summers, Martin. "'Suitable Care of the African When Afflicted with Insanity': Race, Madness, and Social Order in Comparative Perspective." *Bulletin of the History of Medicine* 84 (2010), 58–91.

Sundin, Josefin, Nichole T. Fear, Amy C. Iversen, Roberto J. Rona, and Simon Wessely. "PTSD after Deployment to Iraq: Conflicting Rates, Conflicting Claims." *Psychological Medicine* 40 (2010), 367–382.

Sutker, Patricia B., and Albert N. Allain Jr. "Assessment of PTSD and Other Mental Disorders in World War II and Korean Conflict POW Survivors and Combat Veterans." *Psychological Assessment* 8 (1996), 18–25.

Taber, Katherine H., and Robin A. Hurley. "OEF/OIF Deployment-Related Traumatic Brain Injury." *PTSD Research Quarterly* 21 (2010), 1–7.

Tick, Edward. *Warrior's Return: Restoring the Soul after War.* Boulder, CO: Sounds True, 2014.

Trotti, Michael A. "What Counts: Trends in Racial Violence in the Postbellum South." *Journal of American History* 100 (2013), 383–384.

US Department of Veterans Affairs. "Suicide among Veterans and Other Americans, 2001–2014." Office of Suicide Prevention, August 2016.

Vinovskis, Maris A. "Have Social Historians Lost the Civil War? Some Preliminary Demographic Speculations." In Maris A. Vinovskis, ed., *Toward a Social History of the American Civil War: Exploratory Essays.* New York: Cambridge University Press, 1990.

Warren, Craig A. *The Scars to Prove It: The Civil War Soldier and American Fiction.* Kent, OH: Kent State University Press, 2009.

Weaver, John C. *Sadly Troubled History: The Meanings of Suicide in the Modern Age.* Montreal: McGill-Queen's Press, 2009.

Wimmer, Larry T. "Reflections on the Early Indicators Project: A Partial History." In Dora L. Costa, ed., *Health and Labor Force Participation over the Life Cycle.* Chicago: University of Chicago Press, 2003.

Winter, Jay. "Shell Shock." In Jay Winter, ed., *The Cambridge History of the First World War.* 3 vols. New York: Cambridge University Press, 2014.

Worth, Robert F. "What If PTSD Is More Physical Than Psychological?" *New York Times*, June 10, 2016.

Young, Allan. *The Harmony of Illusions: Inventing Post-Traumatic Stress Disorder*. Princeton, NJ: Princeton University Press, 1997.

Ziff, Katherine K. *Asylum on the Hill: History of a Healing Landscape*. Athens: Ohio University Press, 2012.

Zuckerman, Michael. "The Irrelevant Revolution: 1776 and Since." *American Quarterly* 30 (1978), 224–242.

Index

Index

Lightning Source UK Ltd.
Milton Keynes UK
UKHW020900110819
347774UK00022B/503/P

9 781107 589957